MY BROTHER'S KEEPER

How To Heal America With
The Power of Prayer

A Prescription

Karin E. Offik

KEEPER PUBLISHING
HUNTSVILLE, ALABAMA

ISBN-978-0-9838134-1-5

CONTENTS

Preface

*...all the days ordained for me were written
in Your book before one of them came to be.*[1]

I am a lover of God's Word. I read it every day, day after day, week after week, month after month, and year after year, ever since 1969, the year of my conversion. I prefer it to all other books, for my Lord is in the Word, for He is the Word; and He created the Word. When I read His Word, I am filled with living energy. Joy and peace envelop me. My days are brighter. My nights are sweeter. I can never get enough of it; and no other book can compare to it. Perhaps for this reason, for I have no other real explanation, God took me on a very personal journey with Him at the start of 1998. This book is the result of that journey.

I wrote this story as I lived it, day by day, entering each day's thoughts and activities into an electronic journal. When printed out, this journal produced over 1,500 single-spaced hardcopies, which filled 16 one-and-a-half inch binders. In addition, during my prayer hour, I kept a handwritten journal, of which there are 12 of 150 pages each. Through these daily journal entries, God guided me in the writing of *My Brother's Keeper*. As He brought verses of Scripture, interesting articles, embossed messages or words, stories from other people, communications from friends and so forth, everything became important because everything was lit up with His presence.

Along the way there were many interruptions, countless attacks from the Adversary, numerous drafts, rewrites, and "final versions." I despaired many times and thought this book would never see an end. What started out as a very long book, has become a very short one instead. In the end, God made me aware that the *result* of the journey overshadowed the *process* of the journey.

This book can only be dedicated to One person, and that Person is the Lord Jesus Christ. Especially during the main part of this ten-year journey, during the first three and a half years, the period I refer to as "the whirlwind," God's presence was never so real, nor so sweet. He became my All-in-All, my Constant Companion, and my Ever-Present Joy.

I was truly privileged to walk in His steps in a way I never thought possible. I was blessed to know something about "the

Acknowledgements

I wish to thank the following for their helpful comments, invaluable support, and loving encouragement (listed in the order of their special support):

Joyce Phillips

Mary Jane Brooks

Ohlvia Matheussen

Brenda Karr

Helen Cole

Dinah Williams

Introduction

Is time running out? Are we at the precipice of the end of the age? Is it too late for us to busy ourselves in prevailing prayer for those around us? And what is *prevailing* prayer exactly and for whom should that prayer be offered at this time in the history of our country?

In addition to our economic and financial decline, most Christians would agree that our country is sliding at an alarming rate into immoral chaos. We live in a country that has exchanged technology and materialism for God's Holy Presence. We live in a country in which gross acts of murder and every form of perverse sexual behavior is tolerated. Our philosophy is anything goes, because we don't want to offend anyone. What is worse, sometimes even the most heinous murders often go without a just ending. However, waiting in the wings is a Sovereign Lord who, because of

WHO He is, righteous and holy, must execute judgment against this mode of behavior; in other words, against SIN.

The Old Testament is full of God's righteous execution of justice against all manner of unholy activity—everything from sickness to floods to plagues, death, famine, war, and fire. Here are a few examples:

On floods, hurricanes, and tornadoes: *Therefore, this is what the Sovereign Lord says: In my wrath, I will unleash a violent wind, and in my anger, hailstones and torrents of rain will fall with destructive fury.[1] ...therefore the Lord is about to bring against them the mighty floodwaters of the River (Euphrates).... It will overflow all its channels, run over all its banks....[2]*

On fire: *This is what the Sovereign Lord says: I am about to set fire to you, and it will consume all your trees, both green and dry. The blazing flame will not be quenched, and every face from south to north will be scorched by it. Everyone will see that I the Lord have kindled it; it will not be quenched.[3]*

While there are many disasters to mention, examples of some memorable events include some of the deadliest tornadoes in history, such as those in 2011 that flattened a few cities and towns, including Joplin, Missouri. In 2009, thousands fled their homes from firestorms in Santa Barbara, California. Before that, if one can remember them, since so many floods have happened since then, the Seattle floods. Then there were major ice storms in the

Midwest, again major California firestorms, all in 2007; in 2005, Hurricanes Katrina, Wilma, and Rita, along with tornados in Indiana and Iowa. All of these are strong indications that something is amiss in our country.

In Jeremiah 12:17, God warns all nations not to abandon Him, for *...any nation who refuses to obey me will be uprooted and destroyed. I, the Lord, have spoken.*4 Since God is *the same, yesterday, today, and forever,*5 the fiery judgments of His wrath against evil in ancient times provide grave warnings for us today not to abandon Him. The consequences of abandoning Him will be the same.

Many might dismiss this by saying, "That's the Old Testament. Now we have grace with the New Testament." Yes, God is a God of love, grace, and mercy. He has given us the greatest gift in His Son, Jesus Christ, who died for our sins. We are redeemed in Him. We are rescued from death and hell. But just because God is a God of grace and mercy, does not negate that He is also a God of vengeance, wrath, and judgment against all manner of evil.

Here is what Jesus himself said on this: *Don't misunderstand why I have come. I did not come to abolish the law of Moses or the writings of the prophets. No, I came to fulfill them. I assure you, until heaven and earth disappear, even the smallest detail of God's law will remain until its purpose is achieved.*6

And further: *You have heard that the law of Moses says, 'Do not murder. If you commit murder, you are subject to judgment.' But I say, if you are angry with someone, you are subject to judgment!*[7]

The Father loves his Son and has put everything into his hands. And anyone who believes in God's Son has eternal life. Anyone who doesn't obey the Son will never experience eternal life but remains under God's angry judgment.[8]

With the death of His Son for all of our sins, it is clear that God would rather forgive us than judge us. He said, *There is no judgment against anyone who believes in him.*[9] The task of intercessory prayer by godly Christians can and will prevent God's judgment. God's ear is waiting for our prevailing prayers. He wants to open the hearts of unbelievers and bring them to repentance.

As never before, Christians must exercise their power to pursue God actively in prevailing prayer. This book is about learning how to pray for one person in a prevailing way, how to prepare the soil—the heart—for the entrance of Jesus Christ as Savior and Lord. Prayer is the only answer.

At the most, our faithful, prevailing prayers, as outlined in this book, can redeem our land; and, at the least, they can assure us, the members of Christ's army, that the land has been bathed in prayer, that we have fought and pleaded for its citizens to become members of heaven with rare intensity and steadfastness.

It is possible for things to change in grand fashion. Our country is made up of individuals. Our prayers must be for these individuals who are citizens of these, our United States. One by one, we can make a difference. May this be God's call to action in your prayer life to begin the process of healing our land through the power of prevailing prayer, one for one.

---

[1] Ezek. 13:13, NIV
[2] Isa. 8:7, NIV
[3] Ezek. 20:47, NIV
[4] Jer. 12:17, New Living Translation
[5] Heb. 13:8, NIV
[6] Matt. 5:17-18, NLT
[7] Ibid. 5:21-22
[8] John 3:35-36, NLT
[9] Ibid., 3:18

Am I My Brother's Keeper?
Genesis 4:9, NIV

1

The Fastest Way

What's the fastest way to regain our country's position before God? To regain our health, strength, and peace of mind? To regain a position of true and upright morality? Above all, to avoid God's judgment against the sins of the land?

Today all the television talk shows can easily identify our many and troubling problems. Very often they also deliver appropriate solutions to these problems. But what's missing is the power to get the problems solved. How do we get the power to generate the right actions which will drive the right people to finally administer the appropriate resolutions to the problems? The answer is power. But who has that kind of power? As we all know, it takes much effort by many people to get anything through our bodies of government. But God has immediate power. *For the kingdom of*

God is not a matter of talk but of power.[1] Not only that, He has ALL power. *God made the earth by His power; He founded the world by His wisdom and stretched out the heavens by His understanding.[2]*

God is sovereign. *Everything under heaven belongs to me.[3] With my great power and outstretched arm, I made the earth and its people and the animals that are on it....[4] For every living soul belongs to me, the father as well as the son—both alike belong to me.[5]*

The most important thing to God is the salvation of a soul. It is why Jesus Christ died on the Cross. Conversion work is the work of God. Prayer prepares the ground.

As mentioned in the Preface, God began a very personal journey with me in early 1998 that would reveal as never before the importance of intercessory prayer as the remedy for God to act on our behalf in the redeeming and healing of this land. In the journey I "relearned" what it meant to be a Christian. I "relearned" what it meant to pray in a prevailing, intercessory way as never before. I learned this lesson through friendship; or I should say, the loss of it.

To begin with, I'm a deeply feeling person. I care deeply for all the individuals God has entrusted into my environment, so friendship is important to me. Sometimes one is fortunate, as I have been, to know and enjoy more than one wonderful friend. But making a friend is one thing, keeping one is another. It has always been my belief that once a friend has been made, that friend is a friend for life regardless. Fortunately for me, my friends share this same belief.

My friends are the thirty-, twenty-, ten-year kind of friends. Each has been a priceless and inestimable blessing in my life. But through circumstances and life changes, rather than through any distance of the heart, I had grown apart from most of my friends. Husbands had retired. Grandchildren were underfoot. The rhythm of our lives had changed, and I found myself suddenly lonely.

Twenty-five years before, in 1973, with the death of my father, I had returned home from my National Missionary work with Stonecroft Ministries to join my mother and sixteen-year old brother in the small business my engineer father had established after the demise of the space program in Huntsville, Alabama, where we lived. Our life together was comfortable and good, but while my mother was a faithful and devoted friend, I yearned for a fellowship my mother couldn't give me.

Though I had other prayer partners, from 1974 until 1984, until I worked too far away from our homes to continue our time, my friend Mackie and I prayed together nearly every Thursday morning as prayer partners. Happily married and the mother of three, Mackie never failed to pray for that special man to come into my life, "a life partner."

Though I had had three proposals of marriage from three different men, I had been engaged only once during my college days, but my fiancé Nick had died, and this, tragically. At his home in London, England, several of his doctor friends had asked him to participate in a new experimental drug program. The drug was LSD, and, like Art Linkletter's daughter, it was too much for him. Even as she took her own life, so Nick took his own life. It took years for me to resolve this, for it implied he didn't love me. But I knew in time it wasn't because he didn't love me, but because of the drug. The drug had killed him. Once or twice, I thought Mackie's prayer would come true. But in the end, it didn't.

Since I worked in an area of town where it was difficult even to meet friends for lunch, I was delighted to have found a new friend at my place of work, someone to enjoy a few moments of good conversation, to have an occasional lunch with, and in general enjoy the fellowship I missed with my longtime friends. I met T. in late 1997. She was a software developer, and I was a technical editor for Lockheed Martin, a contractor to the National Aeronautics and Space Administration—NASA—in the Space Shuttle program. In a short period of time, T. and I found we could laugh easily together and share many good conversations. Her reactions to many things were identical to mine.

However, over the next three months, several get-togethers would bring our newly formed friendship into one of great strain.

Even though T. had attended three of the regular Bible study sessions I guided during lunch time at our place of work, I knew her lifestyle was at odds with her expressed desire to return to the Lord. I knew she had made a decision for Christ as a young person, but I also knew she traveled with her boyfriend to other states and countries.

At her first Bible study she asked, "Can you lose your salvation?" At her third, and last, she kept her head down the entire time. A co-worker of hers commented, "She never looked up. Not once!" At the end of the session, after I completed my prayers for everyone's needs, she fled from the room as if on fire.

While our friendship had begun well, with much laughter and good conversation, the spiritual aspect soon brought a distance I was unable to overcome. In the beginning, I wasn't sure if it was only the spiritual or something else, so I made several efforts to learn from T. why her behavior had become so reticent. But she was unwilling to discuss it with me, so the distance spanned the entire time in which we knew each other, from late 1997 to early 2001, when T., along with 26 other employees, was laid off due to Lockheed Martin's downsizing.

On her very last day at work, during her checkout process, God allowed me a final confirmation about this distance. I had just returned from lunch with a co-worker friend when our security officer and T. passed by me inside the foyer of our building. I said

"Hello, T.," but she did not answer. Later, our security officer, herself a Christian, said T. had told her that of all the people she didn't want to see that day, it was me. "She's too religious!"

As a result of this turn of events, God began this special journey with Him in which several important things happened.

First, He led me into isolation with Himself. *There are times and places where God will form a mysterious wall around us, and cut away all props, and all the ordinary ways of doing things, and shut us up to something Divine, which is utterly new and unexpected, something that old circumstances do not fit into, where we do not know just what will happen, where God is cutting the cloth of our lives on a new pattern, where He makes us look to Himself.* [6]

Second, He led me into intense and deep intercessory prayer, a kind I had not known before in all my 30 years of living a dedicated Christian life. As a former missionary, prayer had always been, and still is, the anchor in my relationship with the Living God in the Person of Jesus Christ. Prayer is my balsam, my action to learn God's answer to every need, every question, every opportunity, every hurt. Now God was calling me to something more.

As I began to pray with great strength for this friend, I found myself entering into the most intensely sweet and personal encounter with Him as well. It was during this time, that He began to lead me to write *My Brother's Keeper*; and, as He guided me, every fiber of my being was drawn intensely to His call, His work, His relationship to me, so that nothing else interested me. Even at night, I sometimes awakened with some new insight into a Scripture or something else God revealed that day, and so the entire period was sealed with God's peace and wonderful encouragement.

Third, He allowed me to know something about the hidden realm of the rulers of darkness. I had scant knowledge of them, though I knew they existed. On occasion, I had struggled against them in prayer, but now I would deal with them first hand. *For our struggle is not against flesh and blood, but against the rulers, against the authorities, against the powers of this dark world and against the spiritual forces of evil in the heavenly realms.* [7]

In the beginning, I was unable to discern the great battle I was about to enter. Yes, I was disappointed over the loss of a friend, but I knew I had within me the capacity to overcome this loss quickly by accepting it as coming from the Lord, yet as a great and inexplicable sweep of pain drove through me at odd moments nearly each and every day for over two years, I experienced something I could not describe. I had never known such a pain before. Sometimes, as I felt its approach, I would brace myself, anticipating the blow, then plead the blood of Christ over me all the more earnestly as I felt it sear through my heart like a burning lava. Shortly after its cessation, God restored me to perfect peace. *Spiritual force is stored in the depths of our being, through the very pain which we cannot understand.*[8] Near the end of this two-year cycle, I would learn that others who had similar close encounters with God also suffered similar pains and afflictions.

Fourth, God showed me something about patience in a way I never dreamed necessary. Both old and new friends alike have on occasion stated I am an extremely patient person. That God should come in on this line, a line of strength, would prove how very much I had to learn to depend upon Him. I learned that to wait in quiet patience for something God has promised is one of life's greatest stresses. Early in the journey, in numerous ways, God convinced me a reconciliation and testimony would come at His perfect time. The only question was, "When?"

Yea, I have spoken it, I will also bring it to pass; I have purposed it, I will also do it.[9]

Yes, I would have to be patient. No matter how long it would take—whether a year or two or ten or twenty—I would have to wait and watch and be patient. God's plan would unfold, for God always keeps His promises.

My journey to prepare the ground of my friend's heart began in January 1998. Prayer is a work, and I knew this was my work—to pray in a persistent, prevailing way for God to prepare T.'s heart for salvation in Jesus Christ. No efforts on my part could make this happen. Only God in answer to my prayers could make this happen. It was the fastest and only way.

[1] I Cor. 4:20, NIV
[2] Jer. 10:12, NIV
[3] Job 41:11, NIV
[4] Jer. 27:5, NIV
[5] Ezek. 18:4, NIV
[6] Mrs. Charles E. Cowman, *Streams in the Desert* (Grand Rapids, MI: Zondervan Publishing House, 1977), entry for April 5
[7] Eph. 6:12, NIV
[8] Mrs. Charles E. Cowman, *Streams in the Desert*, entry for March 23
[9] Isa. 46:11, King James Version

2
Greater Love Has No Man

Greater love has no man than this,
that he lay down his life for his friends.¹

Anything of great value is worth fighting for, and so I began to fight for the redemption of this work friend. God had inspired me with a prayer, and I began to pray it faithfully each and every day. I had seen the lovely side of her. I knew God wished to use that side for Himself. It is a side filled with goodness and kindness and great gentleness. But it is at war with another side of her. A dark, emotional side—the side that rejected me without explanation. T. was responding to life around her by the authority of someone other than the Living God. She was not under the influence of Jesus Christ but of the power of the devil, *who walks about like a roaring lion, seeking whom he may devour.²*

Through my earnest prayers, I prevailed upon God to rescue her from the devil's trap, for the Lord *hears the prayers of the righteous,*3 and, *it may be that God will give them the opportunity to repent and come to know the truth. And then they will return to their senses and escape from the trap of the devil who had caught them and made them obey his will.* 4

Our lives are made up of time. Time is life. Time is a gift. Sacrificing time to a friend is the same as laying down your life for a friend. By laying down time, by setting aside the minutes of your life for a friend, you are sacrificing your time, you are giving a portion of your life to that person. *Offer yourselves as a living sacrifice to God, dedicated to His service, and pleasing to Him.*5

If a person gives you their time that is the greatest gift. My gift of friendship to T. would be the gift of my spending time in prayer for her. I would reserve twenty minutes a day to bring this one soul, this one ordinary life to the attention and care of an extraordinary, all-powerful God, a God who would in the end, prove His unbelievable power in the process of changing a life.

Although nothing can ever equal the great sacrifice our Lord Jesus Christ made by physically giving up His life for the atonement of our sins, I came to understand that the verse, *Greater love has no man than this, that he lay down his life for his friends,*6 challenges us to lay down our life for a friend by the sacrifice of time. And in 1 John 3:16: *This is how we know what* *love is: Jesus Christ laid down His life for us. And we ought to lay down our lives for our brothers.*[7]

I learned it was God's intent to bring this ordinary woman into an extraordinary relationship with Himself. He had designs on T. to become an extraordinary woman, and the way He would do it was through my prayers. *See the extent of the love of the children of men to one another. The highest proof of it is laying down one's life for a friend, to save his life. It is love in the highest degree, which is strong as death.*[8]

James 5:16 tells us how to pray: *...the effectual fervent prayer of a righteous man availeth much.*[9] James says to pray with fervency. God wants righteous men and women to come before Him with a fervent heart. What is fervency? It is intense emotion. Intense love. Intense feeling. It is caring fiercely. It is that that is so important to God. He wants to know if we mean business. God wants us to be persistent: *...be persistent in prayer, and keep alert as you pray, with thanks to God.*[10]

Here is the prayer I prayed:

"Dear Lord,

"Forgive me for all my sins, my failures, and my shortcomings. I am only a weak human being. A sinner saved by grace. Thank you for your grace. Thank you for your mercy. Thank you for putting up with me. Thank you that you sent your Son, Jesus Christ, to die for me. Thank you that all my wrong thoughts, motives, desires, and anything else that might be out of joint, is contained in the wounds of Jesus Christ.

"Thank you that your grace is sufficient. Thank you that you made me and thank you for the way in which you made me. I cannot change myself. I can only ask you to change me into the person you would like me to be, and I give you free reign to do so. Thank you that you are a prayer-hearing and a prayer-answering God. Thank you that you are the God of the impossible and the God of the individual.

"Thank you for T. Thank you for bringing her into my life so that I might pray for her. I claim T. for the kingdom of heaven. Prepare her heart to hear the message of Jesus Christ. I pray you will give her the desire to attend a good church where the Word of God is preached. Give her the ability to understand your message, open her mind to it. Ignite her heart and mind with your Word. Build a fire in her soul, a longing to hear your Word and obey it.

"I ask you, Lord to cover T. and her mother and brother with the blood of Jesus Christ. Bind up the unseen rulers of the universe, those spiritual powers of darkness that are in competition with you. Lord, you have authority over every living thing and of all the spiritual forces in high places. BIND THEM UP! Send them into the sea, as you sent the legion of demons into the pigs. Free these individuals from any bondage to these evil forces. They have nothing in her or in her family, and I renounce them in the name of the Living God, Jesus Christ.

"I ask that you bless T. and her family abundantly above all I could ask or think. I ask that you guide their thoughts, their hearts, and their ways. We each desire success and a good family life. I pray that you will give T. and her family the proper perspective of what is truly right living, what is truly success, which is living first for you and second for others, and third for self. May you bring peace to T. and her family as a result of coming to believe that. Give T. and her family the power to surrender themselves into your hands; give them the desire to let go of their lives so that you can take over.

"May your knowledge and wisdom infuse their minds, their souls and their hearts and bring them to the place where you have ordained for them to be. May their lives come to reflect the power and the love of Jesus Christ, because you have a plan for their lives.

"You are an all-powerful God. You are the Master of the Universe. You are GOD ALMIGHTY and no one can go against you. All things are in your hands, and I pray this prayer, knowing you have heard it, and knowing you will answer.

"I expect you to act! I believe you will touch T.'s heart and mind. Thank you in advance for releasing her and her family into the power of your Son, the Living God, Jesus Christ. Thank you for the blessings you have planned! In the name of the Living God, Jesus Christ and in His name, I pray. Amen and Amen."

In praying this prayer, I began to understand more than ever what the verse, *my brother's keeper*, meant. *My brother's keeper*. Not Cain's attitude of keeping his brother, which was malicious envy turned murderous, but God's way. Sacrificial love and care. The great 17th century commentator, Matthew Henry, in commenting on Cain's attitude, said this:

Those who are unconcerned in the affairs of their brethren, and take no care, when they have opportunity, to prevent their hurt in their bodies, goods, or good name, especially in their souls, do, in effect, speak Cain's language.[11]

1 Peter 5:2 clearly states the responsibility we have toward each other: *Be shepherds of the flock that God gave you, and look after it willingly.*[12] And James 5:19, which I believed would eventually prove most appropriate for my friend:

My brothers! If one of you wanders away from the truth, and another one brings him back again, remember this: Whoever turns a sinner back from his wrong ways will save that sinner's soul from death, and bring about the forgiveness of many sins.[13]

3

In His Steps

To this you were called, because Christ suffered for you, leaving you an example, that you should follow in His steps.[1]

From the beginning, I knew T. and her boyfriend were having problems, so I knew she was not a happy woman. But from the beginning, too, I felt identified with her. I felt her pain; I felt her struggles. God was allowing me a window view into her heart and soul. I could feel her stress, her fears, her regrets, and her sorrow. When the deeper prayers for intercession began, I was unaware I would be so identified with T. that I would experience many of her conflicts and her emotional ups and downs.

Jesus would have died for just ONE soul. I was praying for just ONE soul (in addition to my other prayers). When Jesus asked who touched Him, the disciples thought it was a strange question.

37

However, Jesus felt strength leaving Him. He knew someone had drained Him of power. And so it was with me, for as I prayed against the demons, against the Unseen Rulers of the Spirit World, I felt strength leaving me. I exerted *all* my influence in prayer by shouting at these demons to flee! I was so angry when I saw them pressing down on T.! It left me exhausted, but God continued to draw such fiery and compelling prayers from me. He gave me the strength and power to do it.

Two supreme spiritual principals apply in this work. First, the goal of God the Father is to create brothers and sisters for Jesus Christ. As we are being made into the image of His Son, we, too, must bear about in our bodies the pain and suffering of those around us. We must bear their pain, their struggles, their shortcomings. We must bear with them, uphold them, be their rearguard. While we "bear them about in our bodies," we will grow in intimacy with Jesus, for He is the prime example of bearing about in His body all of our sins and shortcomings. This identification has supreme value, then, for us.

In addition, the unsaved individual being prayed for, or the wandering brother or sister in Christ, is God's choice to make into an extraordinary person, the one who exemplifies the sinner on the run from God. T. is an example of someone running from God. She runs from Him, hides from Him, maintains a stubborn posture toward Him, but finally, at some undetermined point in time, will surrender to Him, as He shows her the error of her ways.

As I felt the oppression of those dark forces take hold, I began to fast again on a weekly basis. I had fasted years ago on a regular basis but had not done so recently, and as I fasted and prayed, my identification with T. intensified so much that I even assumed her personality at odd times. I became changeable, as she is changeable. I became short-tempered, as she is short-tempered. I was not myself. On a daily basis, I felt my moods go way down, then way up, then way down again. I was on a roller coaster with no place to stop.

In all my years of Christian life, despite major occurrences such as death in the family, major surgeries, loss of job, struggles in our family business, etc., my bearing was consistent and stable. Now I was experiencing an emotional furnace of such proportions I felt myself sinking underground. Suddenly I would be overwhelmed with moodiness; just as suddenly the moodiness would lift. Only later, by God's revelation, did I realize I was living out the doubts, despair, and pain that conviction by God creates. I understood anew what it meant to be lost, to be searching, to be in pain. It had been thirty years since I had lived through my own conversion. I had lost touch with the relief which true deliverance from darkness brings.

My mood swings were confirmed by a new co-worker friend who said she felt I was "unhappy" and "unapproachable" when she first met me. But I am just the opposite: *Happy and approachable.* For years that has been my reputation. Even my mother said, "I've never known you to be so changeable!"

As my prayers intensified, the demons that held T. prey, were returning to shift their attention back on me. Through my emotions, through my will, through my pain, these spirits waged war against me. I felt myself trying to climb through a deep mire; I wanted desperately to return from the lower depths of the earth.

For we are not fighting against human beings, but against the wicked spiritual forces in the heavenly world, the rulers, authorities, and cosmic powers of this dark age.[2]

Through these painful struggles with the demons, I learned the most important lesson about prevailing intercessory prayer. In the beginning, I had failed to plead the blood of Jesus Christ over myself. I did it for T., but not for myself. That is why they returned to me, so they could vent their fury over my prayers for T.'s salvation, for they do not easily surrender their prey. From then on, I never failed to plead the blood of Christ over myself, my family, and all of our possessions. I did the same with T., her family, and all of their possessions.[3]

But as I went through this process, my faith, as everything else, was on a roller coaster. Doubts would quickly put me into despair, but faith just as quickly restored me into God's peace. Believing brings relief; doubt brings despair. When faith comes easily, everything is easy; but when faith comes hard, everything is hard. God drove this fact deep into my heart, that strong unwavering FAITH is God's greatest gift. Believing is better than disbelieving. It seems so easy, doesn't it? Only when the demons are gone! But here is my conclusion:

Feelings are deceptive.

Feelings lead to doubt.

Doubt leads to depression.

Depression leads to despair.

Despair leads to faithlessness.

Faithlessness leads to gloom.

Gloom leads to a wish for death.

Hanging near death paralyzes life.

BUT.....

Believing brings stability.

Stability brings faith.

Faith brings hope.

Hope brings joy.

Joy brings life.

Life brings strength.

Strength brings power.

Power brings peace.

Peace brings godliness.

And God's Word says: *Godliness makes a nation great.*4 The road to recovery is through prayer. By prayer God changes people and then, by God's power, people change things.

As an intercessor, this ONE-for-ONE prevailing work of prayer gave me a view of Jesus Christ such as I have never had before. Scriptures related to conversion and faith became alive in my heart as if I had breathed in their meaning for the very first time. Everything around me was lit up with meaning and purpose. Life itself became more precious.

In this work of intercessory prayer, I had lifted up prevailing prayers to the Ear of the Master, that He might save this ONE woman. I was supporting her, lifting her up, and, in time, Jesus would claim her. In time God would keep His promise to bring T. to the perfect place—the place of honor before God, joining the Royal Priesthood, standing with Jesus, as a sister to Him.

---

[1] 1 Pet. 2:21, NIV

[2] Eph. 6:12, GNB

[3] Pleading the blood of Jesus Christ over one's self and others, including possessions, in order to obtain the full protection of God's Holy Spirit, is something I have experienced throughout my Christian life. I am aware this is a controversial issue with some Christians, but it was and is a part of my journey with God, and I felt I should share it. I believe it is a powerful tool for Christians to pray in this way whenever and however one is led. Numerous books are available in Christian bookstores that explain this spiritually and scripturally.

[4] Prov. 14:34, NLT

4

The Delay: It's Just a Matter of Time or The Making of a Miracle

A miracle is something extraordinary, something out of the ordinary. Webster's dictionary defines it this way: "An event that seems impossible to explain by natural laws and so is regarded as supernatural in origin or as an act of God."

Natural law says if someone rejects you over a long period of time there is little or no hope there will ever be a reconciliation. We expect that which we see, that which constitutes a set of actions and reactions that convinces us a certain behavior will happen based on those previous instances of behavior.

A watched pot never boils. Some of the old clichés are true, that's why they became clichés. The truth is our eyes must be so focused on God that we will be truly unaware when the promise suddenly springs forward into reality. We will be surprised after all. It is a strange contradiction in God's spiritual school that while we are believing, we are also letting go. We should be firmly anchored in the thing we believe Him for, but also hanging loose, so to speak; waiting patiently and not focusing on the object to be received by faith, but on God who will supply when ready.

While we are fixed with firmness, we are letting go. We hold firm, but we hang loose. Human beings must hinder God by this hanging on because whenever we are too focused on the something which is to happen, it doesn't seem to happen. When we are willing to let go completely, it comes back to us. It is holding on while letting go. It is believing to the end, not giving up, but letting go for God to work. Another cliché says simply: "It happened when I least expected it."

Later I learned something even more important, that letting go is simply just a matter of learning how to be still. To let go means to be still. That sounds easy, but I spent the better part of this journey learning how to be still; and I'm still working on it. In stillness is strength. God breaks through when we are still. *Be still and know that I am God.*[1]

"I know the testimony will come, it's just a matter of time," my friend Maureen had written in an e-mail. Over thirty years ago, this woman, my sister in Christ, had been instrumental in the two most important decisions of my life. First, by inviting me to hear a testimony at a Christian Women's Club (CWC) luncheon, I accepted Jesus Christ that night as my Savior. Second, months later, by taking me to Atlanta for a CWC conference, I accepted God's call to become a National Missionary with the international Christian organization, Stonecroft Ministries.

It's just a matter of time. I knew it was true, but how long was this "matter of time" going to be? *There is a time for everything, and a season for every activity under heaven.*[2]

The time problem began to fascinate me anew. I pondered everything that came my way, such as the following: *...the delay is just as much an answer to your prayer as is the fulfillment when it comes.*[3] I wondered about that. How was the delay working toward the fulfillment? Over the next few months, I began to understand more and more about the need for the delay, as well as God's work in the delay. The two were more closely related than I ever dreamed possible. Here are my conclusions:

In the delay God uses time to fulfill the vision. We know that God can establish instant fulfillment from one day to the next, but He usually doesn't work that way. Nothing happens overnight. We

47

must be *ready*, and we must be *prepared* for the coming of the vision.

God's word to the prophet Habakkuk about the punishment of Babylon took 70 years to become fulfilled. God's instruction was for Israel to wait. *For the revelation awaits an appointed time; it speaks of the end and will not prove false. Though it linger, wait for it; it will certainly come and will not delay.*[4] "Will not delay" translated into 70 years of waiting. Why 70 years? First, because God used that time to discipline Israel for its disobedience to Him. He wanted them to remember that their Babylonian captivity was the result of their disobedience. God had used Israel's enemy to bring judgment against Israel's many sins, especially their worship of false idols. Later He would punish Babylon for their hideous practices and violent sins against His chosen people, Israel. Second, that is how long it took to arrange things to become right and ripe for the fall of Babylon to proceed according to God's decree. Everything went according to God's appointed time, according to His perfect schedule.

Right and Ripe are how things must be before any vision of God can be brought to fruition. We must be right with God first, then we must be ripe in our desire to serve God.

The delay can be better categorized as the instrument through which God brings results. A delay is made up of time. God is the author of time. He is never in a hurry, for He has eternity at His front and at His back. They are one and the same. We run on a different clock. We have a beginning and an end. We increment our life in parcels of time. God does no such thing. The instrument of time is encapsulated with the necessary delay to bring to pass the outcome. Success comes through the slow weaving of time, through the placement of events that produce the actions that finally lead to the decisions that eventually fulfill the vision.

It is the delay that changes the perspective. The perspective is changed through a process of events, one building upon another, until all the events are so arranged so as to produce the desired response. The threads come together "suddenly" in a grand tapestry. When we look back on it, we see the powerful work of God hidden in that tapestry, knowing He has worked it all together for good.

Everything is by degrees. By degrees, the persecution of the demons lifted. By degrees, the turning of events moved the vision forward. Only by degrees. God is building the way. God is building the way by degrees through the use of the delay. At the moment of completion, we are apt to say: "It's a miracle!" And it is, but the delay and the miracle are one and the same.

This working out of the miracle over time is where the strain comes in. We think it is never going to happen. We wait and wait and wait. God keeps us patient. We wait some more. Again we think it is never going to happen, but when the final moment comes, when the miracle is complete, we see the result and think it is a *sudden* happening; it is not. It has been worked on over time to get to a point, and when the point has arrived, the miracle is acknowledged. All of a sudden, it is here. All of a sudden, it is completed. Done. Finished. Now the miracle has arrived. The vision has been made real. "It's a miracle!" A delay is a miracle in progress.

Be glad about this, even though it may now be necessary for you to be sad for awhile because of the many kinds of trials you suffer. Their purpose is to prove that your faith is genuine. Even gold, which can be destroyed, is tested by fire; and so your faith, which is much more precious than gold, must also be tested, that it may endure.[5]

Be still. Expect. Endure.

For in due season, we will reap, if we do not lose heart.[6]

In the beginning, I had wished for a new friend, someone to have lunch with, someone to have fellowship with. At journey's end, a few years later, God had brought me so many new friends and returned so many old friends that suddenly my lunch calendar overflowed. God somehow always makes up to us, and this in abundance.

Finally, the time had come to give thanks to God for the coming victory.

[1] Ps. 46:10, NIV
[2] Eccles. 3:1, NIV
[3] Mrs. Charles E. Cowman, *Streams in the Desert* (Grand Rapids, MI: Zondervan Publishing House, 1977), entry for May 12
[4] Hab. 2:3, NIV
[5] 1 Pet. 1:6-7, GNB
[6] Gal. 6:9, NKJV

5

A Prayer of Thanksgiving

In everything give thanks, for this is
the will of God for you in Christ Jesus.[1]

' Praising God for an answer yet to come is a testimony to the power of God within us. It is always by His grace and always in His strength and always for His glory.

"Lord,

"Today I want to thank you for all that you've done in these last few years. I want to thank you for the whirlwind that began this journey with you that would prove to be so important in my life. I want to thank you for your daily comfort by providing many, many signs and wonders. I want to thank you for the faithful encouragement you gave me through your Word and through the kindness of friends and even strangers.

"You are a faithful God, without fault, and without deceit of any kind. You are not like us—shiftless, moody, or changeable. You are always '...the same yesterday and today and forever.'[2] And you said of yourself, 'I the Lord do not change.'[3] So I know that you would never lead falsely. You would never say something and then either change your mind or not do it, especially a promise of salvation. You wouldn't so much as *one time* say something and let it be false! You would never make a promise and then not keep it. It would not be in your character to do this. When you make a promise, you keep it no matter how difficult it may seem to our human eyes. You keep your promises! And you never make a promise you don't intend to keep.

"I know your timing is always perfect. You are never before or behind your time, and it really doesn't matter if I understand this or not. I remind myself that your ways are always higher than our ways, and I know that no day is wasted. Even if it takes years, I know it will be worth the wait.

"I praise you, Lord, for all your goodness and mercy. Thank you for ALL the good things that are coming! Thank you for the fun and laughter and for the adventures you have planned. Thank you for the coming joy! I claim them all by the power of your Holy

Spirit because you always keep your promises. May it all be to your Glory and Honor! Thank you in Jesus name. Amen."

---

[1] I Thess. 5:18, NKJV
[2] Heb. 13:8, NIV
[3] Mal. 3:6, NIV

The Goal Of
Intercessory Prayer

6

The Expectation of a Testimony

*...there will be more joy in heaven over one sinner who repents
than over ninety-nine just persons who need no repentance.*[1]

This is a short overview of the purpose of this book. It is a
placeholder, if you will, of a future testimony; in my case, the
testimony of the friend for whom I so earnestly prayed.

*The foundation of Christianity is repentance. Strictly
speaking, a person cannot repent when he chooses—repentance is
a gift of God. The old Puritans used to pray for the gift of tears.*[2]

The desire to change must precede the admission of sin, and
God convicts of sin. He gives us the *gift of tears*. What an awesome
thing, to be able to cry, to mourn over our fallen state. In this

condition, we hang precariously between heaven and hell. But in one delicate moment, in one single instance, the balance of our life is changed, for tears are good. They summon an almighty God, whose ear has been bent in our direction, waiting for that cry—*a broken and a contrite heart, O God, you will not despise.*3

Tears are the jewels of the eyes that herald redemption. Tears bring the miracle of redemption to us. They bring forth the birth of new life. When we are born physically the first time, we cry after we leave our mother's womb. We must also cry to receive our second birth, our birth from above, from heaven. If the heart has been truly repentant, truly sorry, God will restore us by the power of His Son, Jesus Christ, who died for each and every one of those sins. *For it is by grace you have been saved, through faith—and this not from yourselves, it is the gift of God—not by works, so that no one can boast.*4 A simple prayer for a sinner's redemption could go like this:

"Dear Lord, I know I've sinned against you, and I am sorry for all the sins I've committed. Thank you that there is forgiveness through your Son, Jesus Christ, who died for all my sins both past and present. I ask you, Jesus, to come into my heart as Savior and Lord, so I can receive your Holy Spirit and begin a new life. And now, I thank you, Lord, for answering this prayer by coming into my heart. Amen."

After the acceptance of Jesus Christ as Savior, we become born again, for Jesus said, *"Flesh gives birth to flesh, but the Spirit gives birth to spirit. You should not be surprised at my saying, 'You must be born again.'* [5]

As the new birth takes hold, we will see in a brand new way. God gives us second sight; and we are changed forevermore. *This means that anyone who belongs to Christ has become a new person. The old life is gone; a new life has begun!* [6]

Over the last ten years, I have wondered many times about the actual event of salvation in T.'s heart—how God would bring her to this point and what kind of a testimony she would have. I longed many times for God to choose me in leading her to make that decision, for I would have considered it my highest privilege, yet I knew God would choose whomever and whatever way would most glorify Him. No one knows where the Spirit of God goes. It is as *the wind (that) blows wherever it wishes; you hear the sound it makes, but you do not know where it comes from or where it is going. It is the same way with everyone who is born of the Spirit.* [7]

I look forward to hearing from this friend. I've been asked by those who have read earlier drafts of this book, "Have you heard from T.?" and I'm always sorry to say, "Not yet." Why God has not yet provided her testimony, is something I cannot answer, but this one thing I know for sure: This person has been prayed for in a prevailing and persistent way. She and her family have been solidly and faithfully covered in prayer in the manner in which God has ordained. I've done my part. I've answered God's call to prayer. And I have been greatly blessed in the process.

Dear reader, may the testimony of the relative, friend, neighbor, or co-worker for whom you are praying, be the genuine vision of your heart. And may God bless you in your waiting.

---

[1] Luke 15:7, NKJV
[2] Oswald Chambers, *My Utmost For His Highest* (Grand Rapids, MI: Discovery House, 1992), December 7
[3] Ps. 51:17, KJV
[4] Eph. 2:8-9, NIV
[5] John 3:6-7, NIV
[6] 2 Cor. 5:17, NLT
[7] John 3:8, GNB

The Second
American Revolution:
Building The Hedge

7

Standing in the Gap

And I looked for a man among them who would
build up the wall and stand before me in the gap
on behalf of the land so I would not
have to destroy it...[1]

During my prayers of intercession for T., I thought, what if each Christian in the United States prays in a persistent, prevailing way for just ONE person who is either unsaved or out of fellowship? What if the prayer for redemption would take only 10 minutes a day and it was prayed for 365 days a year? In actual time that comes to 60 hours or a little more than 2.5 days.

Few, if any, would pray continuously for 2.5 days without sleep, so I spread out the time over an 8-hour work week. Converting 60 hours into a regular workweek of 8 hours a day translated into about one and a half week's worth of effort. Would a man sacrifice one and a half weeks, or 10 days, of his life to redeem one soul from hell, which lasts for eternity? I would think the answer would be a resounding yes!

ONE Christian. ONE sinner. ONE for ONE. Taking the one-for-one praying further, if, after a period of time, up to one year, this sinner becomes a Christian, then both of you can pray for two more souls in the following year. And continuing this pattern, by the end of the 11th year, you will have exponentially delivered to God, 1,024 souls. And it began with ONE!

Let us dream a big dream. Let us chart a scenario that may seem very unrealistic, but let us remember that *What is impossible with men is possible with God.*[2] While our big dream may never be fully answered, at least the bigness of it will deliver some changes that could turn things around in our country.

According to the 2010 U.S. Census, the population of the United States is over 303 million. In this same census, the statistics on one major evangelical Christ-centered denomination is 100 million. This denomination has a total of 41 factions, but for this example, let's take only three factions. Subtracting those members in these three factions who are already committed to Jesus Christ, or 28 million, now leaves a population of 275 million, for whom prayers must be offered. Remember, this is only a small part of one major denomination. The figures become more and more favorable the greater the participation from this denomination's remaining factions plus scores of other Christian denominations. In sum, our dream-like scenario could look something like this:

In the first year, 28 million members of one Christian denomination begin the work of intercession. In the second year, 35 million intercessors, with the possible addition of 7 million. In the third year, 42 million intercessors, with the possible addition of another 7 million. In the fourth year, 49 million intercessors, with the possible addition of another 7 million.

The total number of individuals for whom intercession has been made in these 4 years equals 154 million. Subtracting these 154 million from our goal number leaves a total of 121 million lives left for whom intercession must be made. If the previous scenario is repeated as follows:

In the fifth year, 56 million intercessors, with the possible addition of another 7 million from the fourth year of 49 million. In the sixth year, 63 million intercessors, with the possible addition of another 7 million. In the seventh year, 70 million intercessors, with the possible addition of another 7 million.

The remaining 121 million individuals will have been redemptively prayed for in less than another 3 years, without anyone else from any other denomination joining in.

The one-for-one prayer prayed by these committed Christians would more than cover the entire population of the United States in less than 8 years—or the time of two U.S. presidential terms of office.

It is a fantastic scenario for sure. Only God knows how many will actually come, for we all know the bent of the human heart and its direct opposition to all things spiritual, but at least we know we've covered the ground, and the possibility exists that enough Christians would be born to tilt the scales in God's favor.

The potential for right living that follows true conversion is limitless, provided the Holy Spirit is in control. Everything would be affected because God changes people and people change things: The government, the economy, the legal system, the medical community, the education system, the prison system, the entertainment industry, and, most importantly, our lifestyle—our family life. *So let us not become tired of doing good; for if we do not give up, the time will come when we will reap the harvest.*[3]

Are we living in the end times? Many believe yes. If it is the end of the age, and our land is not redeemed, remember this: Somewhere in the world, in some country, in some town, there exists a man or a woman or a child who will be the last soul saved before Christ's return. That soul might be a citizen of the United States, and on the list of one of those faithful and dedicated 28 million who are committed to prevailing prayer.

To redeem our country, we must take seriously 2 Chronicles 7:14: *If my people, who are called by my name, will humble themselves and pray and seek my face and turn from their wicked ways, then will I hear from heaven and will forgive their sins and will heal their land.*[4]

This Scripture is meant for all of God's people who are called by His name. We are God's people if we bear the name of Jesus Christ. We are Christians. We bear His name. In addition, this Scripture asks us to do the following:

HUMBLE ourselves.

SEEK His face.

TURN from our wicked ways.

PRAY.

As I prayed for T., I took it seriously. I searched my own heart daily on a constant basis to make sure nothing was hidden somewhere deep down, something that could possibly displease God. If I found something, I confessed it, for I wanted to make sure that nothing would hinder my prayers from reaching His Ear.

Our intercessory prayers must be part of our heartbeat. God didn't call unbelievers to live like Christians. He called Christians to live like Christians. Trying to make a moral nation out of immoral people is not the plan. That is legalism. The plan is to make believers out of unbelievers and then allow the Holy Spirit to make changes in how we live. During my special journey, God revealed to me as never before that change can come only from Christians themselves—Christians prevailing in prayer for others; Christians standing in the gap for the lost; and Christians renewing their commitment to Jesus Christ by living the kind of godly lives the Scriptures speak about.

One good example of someone who stood in the gap to prevent God's judgment was Moses. Psalm 106:21-23 (NIV), which is actually a summary of Exodus 32, writes about the idolatrous Israelites:

> *They forgot the God who saved them,*
> *who had done great things in Egypt,*
> *miracles in the land of Ham*
> *and awesome deeds by the Red Sea.*
> *So He said He would destroy them—*
> *had not Moses, His chosen one,*
> *stood in the breach before him*
> *to keep His wrath from destroying them.*[5]

"Sin and its consequences grieve God, who created the world in order to provide grace, not judgment. Though God does not delight in destroying the wicked, He cannot allow sin to go unchecked. If He did, sin would eventually destroy all people and all creation. So, for one who persists in sin, punishment is the final result. But if someone abandons a life of sin, that one can escape punishment.

The choice for judgment or mercy, for death or life, belongs to the wicked."[6]

How then can we bring those who are unsaved to a place where they will choose life? Where they will choose mercy? In Acts 16:14, Lydia fell under the spell of Paul's preaching, and the Lord opened her heart to respond to Paul's message. God opened her heart. During those early days of our Christian beginnings, the apostles prayed much and many hearts were opened.

In addition to our intercessory prayers for ONE individual, we must stir up our hearts to pray for our country as a whole. A good illustration of care and concern for a country is illustrated in Daniel 9.

When Israel disobeyed God with idol worship, He inflicted severe punishment on them by placing them into captivity under their much-feared enemy, Babylon. When Daniel, who had been studying the Scriptures, read the words of Jeremiah,[7] he learned that Israel's captivity under Babylonian rule would last 70 years. This was a great blow to his heart. Immediately, he began to mourn and pray for Israel with great feeling because of the "great disaster" God had brought upon them for their disobedience. It grieved Daniel, and he humbled himself. He stood in the gap for his people and country with this prayer:

"Lord, you are righteous, but this day we are covered with shame—the men of Judah and people of Jerusalem and all Israel, both near and far, in all the countries where you have scattered us because of our unfaithfulness to you. O LORD, we and our kings, our princes and our fathers are covered with shame because we have sinned against you. The Lord our God is merciful and forgiving, even though we have rebelled against him; we have not obeyed the LORD our God or kept the laws he gave us through his servants the prophets. All Israel has transgressed your law and turned away, refusing to obey you.

"Therefore the curses and sworn judgments written in the Law of Moses, the servant of God, have been poured out on us, because we have sinned against you. You have fulfilled the words spoken against us and against our rulers by bringing upon us great disaster. Under the whole heaven nothing has ever been done like what has been done to Jerusalem. Just as it is written in the Law of Moses, all this disaster has come upon us, yet we have not sought the favor of the LORD our God by turning from our sins and giving attention to your truth. The LORD did not hesitate to bring the disaster upon us, for the LORD our God is righteous in everything he does; yet we have not obeyed him.

"Now, O Lord our God, who brought your people out of Egypt with a mighty hand and who made for yourself a name that endures to this day, we have sinned, we have done wrong. O Lord, in keeping with all your righteous acts, turn away your anger and your wrath from Jerusalem, your city, your holy hill. Our sins and the iniquities of our fathers have made Jerusalem and your people an object of scorn to all those around us.

"Now, our God, hear the prayers and petitions of your servant. For your sake, O Lord, look with favor on your desolate sanctuary. Give ear, O God, and hear; open your eyes and see the desolation of the city that bears your Name. We do not make requests of you because we are righteous, but because of your great mercy. O Lord, listen! O Lord, forgive! O Lord, hear and act! For your sake, O my God, do not delay, because your city and your people bear your Name."[8]

Daniel was passionate. He was humble. He cried out to the Lord.

The next chapters provide the prescription necessary to become a true intercessor for God on behalf of the land. It is the way to build a human wall, a human shield—one for one—all around our country from east to west and north to south—every state, every city, every county—to protect and prevent God from executing any further judgments against us.

[1] Ezek. 22:30, NIV
[2] Luke 18:27, NIV
[3] Gal. 6:9, GNB
[4] 2 Chron. 7:14, NIV
[5] Ps. 106:21-23, NIV
[6] *Quest Study Bible,* NIV (Grand Rapids, MI: Zondervan Publishing House, 1994, commentary on Ezekiel 33:11, p.1185)
[7] Dan. 9:2, NIV
[8] Ibid., 9:7-19, NIV

8

Identifying God's Fingerprint: Knowing God

*...the Hand of the Lord will be made
known to His servants.[1]*

Knowing God is the first prerequisite in becoming truly effective in the power of prevailing prayer, but how do we know when God is leading us? As Christians, we have the high privilege of knowing God through our personal relationship with Jesus Christ, but what are the different ways He can speak to us? First and foremost, of course, is through God's Word. God never goes contrary to His own Word. If God's Word says "do thus and so" and you do something else, you are out of God's will. If you are a true child of God, God's Holy Spirit will lead you to agree with His

Word. *We have not received the spirit of the world, but the Spirit who is from God, that we may understand what God has freely given us.*[2] *And this is how we know that God lives in us: we know it because of the Spirit He has given us.*[3]

Especially in the beginning part of this journey, the first three and a half years, God led me not only through His Word, through people, and through circumstances, but by embossed things, such as words, phrases, physical objects, word pictures, and returning themes, as expressed either in His Word or through answered prayers. God allowed me to see first hand His handiwork, His behind-the-scenes operations. God showed me how extraordinary life with Him can be. God's imprints were everywhere. I was delighted by how He energized my daily life with His surprising, often funny, imprints and messages. I came to believe that, like our genetic code, the tapestry of our lives is a work complete upon birth. Seeing God in the little things, experiencing His surprises, getting that lift out of the humdrum activities of the day adds a special dimension to daily life. They are all there, hidden in the background—all the clues, all the signs, all the blessings— but to see the splendor of their weave, we must put on our spiritual glasses in intimacy with Him. We must be sensitive to His leading.

By the end of the journey, God had returned *every scripture, every word, every phrase, every word picture, and every theme* He had used during this three-and-a-half-year period. Everything had a beginning, a middle, and an end. Everything was related, and everything pointed toward salvation. God is in the details. *Not even the smallest detail of life happens unless God's will is behind it. Therefore, you can rest in perfect confidence in Him.*[4]

God's hugs and kisses, as I began to think of them, came to me not because I asked for them. I never asked for them. I never asked for a sign. I never prayed "Lord, give me a sign. Show me something special." Each and every *thing* or *word* or *word picture* that God brought to my attention came by His loving Hand. All around me, as He whispered tender hugs and kisses into my life, He was embracing me with His love. His Living Presence had anointed me with an indescribable love, joy, and peace that made anything and anyone who lived and breathed in the actual, physical world around me, a mere shadow. *So then, men ought to regard us as servants of Christ and as those entrusted with the secret things of God,*[5] *for the Lord confides in those who fear Him.*[6]

In this case, "fear" refers less to "being afraid" than to what our position toward the Sovereign Lord should be. By "fearing" Him, we are giving Him our highest respect, our deepest honor. We are confirming our unwavering and abiding grasp of WHO HE IS. As we do this, as we behold God with awesome wonder, He is surprisingly generous and gracious toward us in return. Then, and only then, will He reveal His secrets to us. What follows are a few examples of the different ways in which God guided me into a more personal and vivid understanding of His presence.

For instance, on a certain day in 1998, when my spirits were sagging, I drove past Maple Hill Cemetery, where my father was buried. I was on my way home. A car passed me. As he sped by me, I noticed his license plate: *Story 2.*

Story 2! It was a magnetic impulse that drew me to the plate; it was a lifting that made me aware it was the Holy Spirit. He was encouraging me to know that the testimony, Part II, was coming. This was confirmed a few minutes later at the home of my mother's friend, where I had stopped for a moment to drop off an item. The first thing out of her mouth was that her daughter's mare had just given birth to a foal they named *Amazing Grace.*

Story 2. Amazing Grace.

One year later, in 1999, confirming again His promise by bringing it full circle, the same thing happened. I was driving away from the shopping center where I had browsed in *Books-A-Million*, after work. Once more nagging doubts filled me with disbelief. As I pulled up to the traffic light, a car in the left lane moved ahead of me. I glanced at the license plate. *Story 2.* At the same time, while still waiting for the traffic light to change, my eyes were magnetically drawn to the word *Harvest* in the company name of Harvest Bread Company, several doors down from *Books-a-Million.*

Story 2. The Harvest! The testimony! My faith was restored.

On another day, while I was fasting, I had spent my lunch hour quietly at the Madison Public Library reading and praying. I was returning to work, praising God out loud in the car. I was in the left-hand lane by *Applebee's* waiting for the traffic signal to change. "Lord," I said joyously, "You are so exciting!" The light had changed, and no sooner had the words left my mouth, when a sports car whizzed by me with the license plate: *EXTNG.*

Perfect timing. This is where God makes Himself real and manifest, where He majestically displays His mighty power. He shows us His power in the *timing* of a thing, for no human being has this kind of power. Who can manage events in a certain way so as to move two individuals together at *the exact precise moment* so that they will coincide at a particular place at a particular time but without either one knowing it? Even when two individuals have planned to meet for lunch or a movie at a certain location, they most often miss each other by a minute or at least a few seconds, coming either too late or too soon, and both individuals have watches that supposedly run on exact time. But God's timing is perfect because He has the power to *count down to the very second* because He knows how long a thing will take, bringing a perfect order and balance to the moment at hand.

Only God's perfect timing could create such a moment. Only by such down-to-the-second timing is it possible to *speak a thought* and *receive a confirmation* instantly after its utterance. Later, I had perfectly timed run-ins with other tags and other people God brought to my attention. Over and over and over.

Once, at work, even my friend Teddy and I had two perfectly timed run-ins at the door to the ladies' room, only minutes apart. In each case, Teddy opened the door from the inside as I opened it from the outside. We laughed as we nearly collided the first time. A short while later, not long, perhaps ten or fifteen minutes, the very same thing happened. As she shook her head in disbelief, Teddy said, "I can't believe this! This doesn't happen!" But it does. With God such things can and do happen all the time. He can bring things together perfectly. It is only up to us to become aware of His workings. *For God may speak in one way, or in another, yet man does not perceive it.*[7]

Are you beginning to believe that God can be exciting? It is all about watching for associations. God communicates through His Word, but He can also come through such intimate associations, through tags that inform us of His plans for our lives. Through such personal confirmations, God assured me of victory. He assured me of the outcome. It was only a matter of time.

The greatest beginning to prevailing prayer is to know God and how He leads us. With an understanding of His personal associations in our lives, we can begin to pray with true depth in our prayers of intercession.

---

[1] Isa. 66:14, NIV
[2] 1 Cor. 2:12, NIV
[3] 1 John 3:24, GNB
[4] Oswald Chambers, *My Utmost For His Highest* (Grand Rapids, MI: Discovery House, 1992), entry for July 16
[5] 1 Cor. 4:1, NIV
[6] Ps. 25:14, NIV
[7] Job 33:14, NKJV

9

Godly Behavior:
The Road to Intercession

Righteousness exalts a nation.[1]

The second prerequisite to a deep prayer relationship with God is to live a godly life. But how do you live a godly life? And what is godly behavior? God commands us to live godly lives. *So then let us purify ourselves from everything that makes body or soul unclean, and let us be completely holy, living in fear of God.*[2] Godly behavior means living differently than the world. *Do not love the world or anything that belongs to the world.*[3]

Each individual Christian should know what requirements are inherent to the Christian lifestyle from studying God's Word, but here are some key points to observe about godly behavior: No lying. *An honest answer is a sign of true friendship.4* No gossiping. *Gossip separates the best of friends.5* No cheating. No sexual perversity. No lascivious dressing (tight pants; short skirts). No mixing of old and new lifestyles. (Leave your old bad habits in the old life. If you don't know what they are, pray for God to show you.)

No coarse or foul language, especially any misuse of God's name. Sometimes I hear well-meaning Christians say "My God!" That is misusing God's name; it is breaking one of His Ten Commandments. *You shall not misuse the name of the Lord your God, for the Lord will not hold anyone guiltless who misuses His name.6*

No "R" or "X" rated movies. Think of input/output: What you put in, you get out. *For as he thinks in his heart, so is he.7 Whatever is true, whatever is noble, whatever is right, whatever is pure, whatever is lovely, whatever is admirable—if anything is excellent or praiseworthy—think about such things. 8*

No condemnation of others. Jesus didn't come to condemn the world, neither should we. *For God did not send His Son into the world to condemn the world but to save the world through Him.9 Do not judge, or you too will be judged. For in the same way you judge others, you will be judged, and with the measure you use, it will be measured to you. Why do you look at the speck of sawdust in your brother's eye and pay no attention to the plank in your own eye?* [10]

Do everything without complaining or arguing, so that you may become blameless and pure, children of God without fault in a crooked and depraved generation, in which you shine like stars in the universe as you hold out the word of life. [11]

Our genetic makeup seems unalterable. We are born with a certain set of genes, and we can't seem to escape from them. Still, through the power of the Holy Spirit, things can happen in an individual's life that can change how we think, feel, and respond to life. Our lives can take on the edge of power, of holiness, of completeness but only through the power of God. I'm just an ordinary person, but my heart is filled with extraordinary things; with vision, purpose, with a love for God made possible only through His Son, Jesus Christ. Extraordinary things come only through Him.

When self is in command of the general handling of life's situations, things may go well or they may not go well, but with God, His way is always perfect, even though it may appear otherwise. *As for God, His way is perfect.* [12]

God wants us to live in *godliness* and show *proper conduct.* A godly life is filled with godly pursuits, pursuits which are clothed with peace, joy, and love of God. That means reading the Word, praying, attending church, and fellowshipping with other

Christians. *When a man's ways please the Lord, He makes even his enemies to be at peace with him.*[13] God rewards and blesses godly living. It opens the way for others to become saved through our prayers, and we all know that in order for our lives to be truly free to live godly lives and enjoy proper conduct, those around us must become godly, too. Weeds choke the life out of flowers, and I know you will agree that it's high time to begin praying as never before for those weeds to be changed into flowers!

Knowing God and living a godly life qualify you to stand in the gap as an intercessor for God in the work of redemption for our land.

---

[1] Prov. 14:34, NIV
[2] 2 Cor. 7:1, GNB
[3] 1 John 2:15, GNB
[4] Prov. 24:26, NIV
[5] Ibid., 16:28, NLT
[6] Exod. 20:7, NIV
[7] Prov. 23:7, NKJV
[8] Phil. 4:8, NIV
[9] John 3:17, NIV
[10] Matt. 7:1-4, NIV
[11] Phil. 2:14-16, NIV
[12] Ps. 18:30, NKJV
[13] Prov. 16:7, NKJV

10

The Basic Structure of Intercessory Prayer

The effective, fervent prayer of a
Righteous man avails much.[1]

Godly men and women have power with God. The true test of a person's position before God is whether or not God answers his/her prayers. God answers the prayers of godly men and women, especially prayers for salvation and the pursuit of godly living.

He listens to the godly man who does His will.[2] To pray, however, we must be *clear minded and self-controlled.* [3]

The first goal is to be heard. Confession opens the gateway. *If I regard iniquity in my heart, the Lord will not hear.*[4] Every prayer should begin with a confession. *But if we confess our sins to God, He will keep His promise and do what is right: He will forgive us our sins and make us clean from all our wrongdoings.*[5]

Once we've sincerely confessed any wrongdoing, God listens. *This is the confidence we have in approaching God: that if we ask anything according to His will, He hears us. And if we know that He hears us—whatever we ask—we know that we have what we asked of Him.*[6]

After confession, comes praise. *It is fitting for the upright to praise Him.*[7] God likes to be praised. He enjoys hearing us thank Him for good news, the good news He creates for us each and every day. Imagine how much bad news God has to put up with every day, the bad news man creates for himself in a world which chooses to live apart from Him, which sides more with Satan than with an all-loving, tender-hearted God. I watch the news every day, but I'd rather not. There are too many terrible things being reported. Imagine God's despair over His first-hand view of all the evil all over the globe, each and every day, day in and day out. Imagine seeing so much anguish, so much tragedy, so much horror. His loving heart surely rends daily in agony over it. *O God, you take no pleasure in wickedness; you cannot tolerate the sins of the wicked,*[8] and *(you) get angry with (them) every day.*[9] It is clear that praise is a balsam to Him; it is music to His ears. Praise comforts and pleases Him. *Whoso offers praise glorifies me.*[10]

Therefore by Him let us continually offer the sacrifice of praise to God, that is, the fruit of our lips, giving thanks to His name.[11]

Following confession and praise, comes the body of the prayer. In the next chapter is a sample of the Prayer of Intercession.

---

[1] James 5:16, NKJV
[2] John 9:31, NIV
[3] 1 Pet. 4:7, NIV
[4] Ps. 66:18, NKJV
[5] 1 John 1:9, GNB
[6] Ibid., 5:14-15, NIV
[7] Ps. 33:1, NIV
[8] Ibid. 5:4, NLT
[9] Ibid., 7:11, NLT
[10] Ibid., 50:23, NKJV
[11] Heb. 13:15, NKJV

11

The Prayer of Intercession

The men who have done the most for God in
this world have been early upon their knees.1

Why pray a formula prayer? When God inspired me with this prayer, I never questioned its validity. I never viewed it as a "formula" prayer. My purpose in praying it was to rescue my friend from Satan's trap. It was to restore her soul to Jesus Christ, to free her from the bondage of the dark demon world, and to prevail upon God to translate her into His Kingdom of Light.

After praying this prayer for five months, day in and day out, I noticed something. I knew God was working to accomplish His perfect will in bringing T. to salvation, but the prayer changed me, too. Others who prayed it, had similar results.

First, it reestablishes a set period of time in which to pray. Consider your current prayer life. Perhaps it is always wonderfully adequate, but, if you're like me, it is not always so wonderful. There are days when I just don't feel like it, days when I seem to repeat myself in ways that bore even me. The words seem to fall asleep on my very tongue! Poor God! So if you've been praying a hasty five- or six-minute prayer here and there, on the run, while getting ready for work, or driving to work, this will carve out a new timeframe. It will create a new habit. A good, strong habit. Once God ends this line of praying, for it begins and ends with Him, the habit of praying in a prevailing way for a longer period of time will have been carved out.

Second, it reestablishes the language of prayer by using words which please God. It isn't necessary to use flowery words. Simple is best, but how many times have you fled your duty in prayer because you couldn't think of a creative way to phrase your thoughts? This prayer revitalizes the language of prayer.

Third, it reestablishes the link to God's power. It is next to impossible to pray successfully for any length of time without the power of the Holy Spirit. When emotions entangle us in self-centered desires, prayers are heavy handed. They lack power. However, when you partner with God in the work of redemption that changes.

Redemption is first of all God's work, *for the battle (is) God's.*[2] God threads His redemptive Voice through our hearts and souls, to pray in line with His will, and salvation is at the top of His list. God directs you, lifts you, and sustains you into a position with Him that rewards you with strength and peace. As you allow Him to fulfill His purpose in prayer through you, God blesses you.

We do not know what we ought to pray for, but the Spirit himself intercedes for us with groans that words cannot express. And he who searches our hearts knows the mind of the Spirit, because the Spirit intercedes for the saints in accordance with God's will.[3]

God's will is for all to be saved. *He is not willing that any should perish but that all should come to repentance.*[4] Jesus said, *Do not be surprised because I tell you that you must all be born again.*[5]

Finding the time to pray the Prayer of Intercession may seem difficult to you, but that is where the sacrifice comes in. If it was easy, it wouldn't be a sacrifice. *No discipline seems pleasant at the time, but painful. Later on, however, it produces a harvest of righteousness and peace for those who have been trained by it.*[6]

Keep the end result before you: You are working *with God* to bring change to ONE person, to redeem ONE person, to bring health and strength to ONE person. You are joining thousands of other Christians across America who are praying in this same way, each praying for the redemption of ONE person. At some point in time, perhaps a year, perhaps two, but several years for sure, the impact of those prayers will become manifest. The change to our country will become visible. Keep that vision. Keep that goal in front of you always as you pray for the redemption of that ONE soul.

This prayer takes about ten minutes to pray, whereas the prayer I prayed for T., took about twenty minutes, due to the different personal aspects I included. After prayerfully seeking God's choice, personalize the prayer by filling in the person's name in the blank lines provided in the prayer of intercession.

Dear Lord,

Forgive me for all my sins, my failures, and my shortcomings. I am only a weak human being. A sinner saved by grace. Thank you for your grace. Thank you for your mercy. Thank you for putting up with me. Thank you that you sent your Son, Jesus Christ, to die for me. Thank you that all my wrong thoughts, motives, desires, and anything else that might be out of joint, is contained in the wounds of Jesus Christ.

Thank you that your grace is sufficient. Thank you that you made me and thank you for the way in which you made me. I cannot change myself. I can only ask you to change me into the person you would like me to be, and I give you free reign to do so.

94

Thank you that you are a prayer-hearing and a prayer-answering God. Thank you that you are the God of the impossible and the God of the individual.

Thank you for _____. Thank you for bringing _____ to my attention so that I might lift (her/him) up to you in prayer. I claim _____ for the kingdom of heaven. Prepare _____'s heart to hear the message of Jesus Christ. I pray you will give _____ the desire to attend a good church where the Word of God is preached. Give _____ the ability to understand your message, open (his/her) mind to it. Ignite (his/her) heart and mind with your Word. Build a fire in (his/her) soul, a longing to hear your Word and obey it.

I ask you, Lord, to cover _____ and (his/her) spouse and (his/her) children with the blood of Jesus Christ. Bind up the unseen rulers of the universe, those spiritual powers of darkness that are in competition with you. Lord, you have authority over every living thing and of all the spiritual forces in high places. BIND THEM UP! Send them into the sea, as you sent the legion of demons into the pigs. Free these individuals from any bondage to these evil forces. They have nothing in (him/her) and (his/her) family, and I renounce them in the name of the living God, Jesus Christ.

I ask that you bless_____ and (his/her) family abundantly above all I could ask or think. I ask that you guide their thoughts, their hearts, and their ways. We each desire success and a good family life. I pray that you will give _____ the proper perspective of what is truly right living, what is truly success, which is living first for you and second for others, and third for self. May you bring peace to _____ and (his/her) family as a result of coming to believe that. Give _____ and (his/her) family the power to surrender themselves into your hands; give them the desire to let go of their lives so that you can take over.

May your knowledge and wisdom infuse their minds, their souls and their hearts and bring them to the place where you have ordained for them to be. May their lives come to reflect the power and the love of Jesus Christ, because you have a plan for their lives.

You are an all-powerful God. You are the Master of the Universe. You are GOD ALMIGHTY and no one can go against you. All things are in your hands. I pray this prayer, knowing you have heard it, and knowing you will answer.

I expect you to act! I believe you will touch _____ heart and mind. Thank you in advance for releasing _____ into the power of your Son, the Living God, Jesus Christ. Thank you for the blessings you have planned! In the name of the Living God, Jesus Christ and in His name, I pray. Amen and Amen.

[1] Mrs. Charles E. Cowman, *Streams in the Desert* (Grand Rapids, MI: Zondervan Publishing House, 1977, entry for March 2)
[2] 1 Chron. 5:22, NIV
[3] Rom. 8:26-27, NIV
[4] 2 Pet. 3:9, KJV
[5] John 3:7, GNB
[6] Heb. 12:11, NIV

Prologue to
The Call to Intercede

America

While the storm clouds gather far across the sea,
Let us swear allegiance to a land that's free,
Let us all be grateful for a land so fair,
As we raise our voices in a solemn prayer.[1]

God bless America,
Land that I love,
Stand beside her and guide her
Through the night with a light from above;

From the mountains, to the prairies,
To the oceans white with foam,

God bless America,

My home, sweet home.

God bless America,

My home, sweet home. [2]

O beautiful for spacious skies,

For amber waves of grain,

For purple mountain majesties

Above the fruited plain!

America! America!

God shed his grace on thee

And crown thy good with brotherhood

From sea to shining sea.[3]

---

[1] *America*, Irving Berlin, introduction to, 1918
[2] *America,* Irving Berling, 1918; revised 1938 (first and second stanzas)
[3] *America the Beautiful*, Katharine Lee Bates, 1893; 2nd version, 1994; final version, 1913 (first stanza)

12

The Call to Intercede

If my people, who are called by my name, will humble themselves and pray and seek my face and turn from their wicked ways, then will I hear from heaven and will forgive their sin and will heal their land.[1]

What is the role of today's Christian? Is it condemnation or sacrifice? Many Christians, myself included, believe God's judgment has already started. Look around you for proof. Just listen to the news. Or look at your lifestyle. Is your life victim to stress, mental unease, and violence? Is your life one of quality or just a rush to make ends meet, flop in your chair at the end of the day to recover yourself for a new onslaught of work and stress the next day? Our lives should reflect God's favor in every respect.

That means our lives should be filled with nurturing relationships both inside and outside our homes. That means our lives should be stable, moral, and productive. And joyful.

Are we, as a people of God, willing to let things morally deteriorate still more? Will we try God's Hand to the point of no return? Or can we stay His hand from severe judgment awhile longer? Can we redeem our land through intercessory prayer? Is it too late? Only God knows, but one thing is sure: The battle cannot be won in any other way but on our knees. All the protests, legalistic actions, petitions, and constant jabbering on talk shows, cannot win this battle. All the talking in the world can't change a human heart. No leader in office can change a human heart. Only God can change a heart; and God changes a heart in response to prayer. *Prevailing prayer.*

This battle can only be fought ON OUR KNEES with the prayers of an upright people, an honorable people, God's people— true men and women of God, men and women who profess Jesus Christ as Savior and Lord and who live godly lives.

While we are waiting for the coming again of Jesus Christ, God the Father is searching the hearts of men and women, looking for intercessors, individuals who are willing to stand in the gap for others, to sacrifice time in prayer before Him, not with ordinary prayer, but with prevailing prayer—*daily, consistent, willful, intense prayer*—focused on a friend or an acquaintance or even a stranger—a pouring out of heart and soul for the one who is headed straight for hell instead of heaven.

Are we complacent? Easy in our easy chairs, happy to know where we are going? Wishing our neighbor would make it, too, but he just doesn't seem to get it? Why won't he wake up, we wonder, while we are watching *The Hallmark Movie*?

And in church, when we sing good gospel songs, like *Onward Christian Soldiers*[2], are we feeling it deeply enough or just mouthing words? *Onward Christian soldiers, marching as to war, with the Cross of Jesus, going on before.* The rhythm is catchy. It is good foot stomping music, and, in that moment of joyous singing, we love our Savior especially much. We feel empowered to do anything in a moment like that. The second verse begins with: *Like a mighty army....* Army? War? We know that. But do we really?

Our country is in a spiritual warfare with the unseen forces of evil. *For our struggle is not against flesh and blood, but against the rulers, against the authorities, against the powers of this dark world and against the spiritual forces of evil in heavenly realms.*[3] If our country continues destroying unborn children (over forty-eight million to date), committing every sexual perversity known to man, deleting God from the court system, the schools, Christmas celebrations, and who knows what else, God will bring the same severe judgment to the land as He did in ancient times. He is the same God today as He was then.

Even worse, we could lose our freedom. The potential loss of freedom in our beloved United States of America should be part of our every waking and praying thought. Don't think the loss of freedom can't happen. The fall from within brings a force from without. The occupation of our land by a foreign country is unthinkable to the American mind, but when God begins to judge as He has judged in days of old, that possibility is chillingly possible. God used Babylon to punish His people Israel with a 70-year captivity because they abandoned Him. It is clear that if a nation abandons God, God will abandon that nation. Many examples exist in the Old Testament that show how God executes judgment against His people when they fail Him and become immersed in the kind of dark quagmire of a culture we are currently steeped in. *Any nation who refuses to obey me will be uprooted and destroyed. I, the Lord, have spoken.4 He makes nations great, and destroys them....5*

In 1956, the U. S. Congress voted that each bill and coin should be imprinted with the phrase *In God We Trust.* Today, if certain individuals had their way, it would read more like*: Let God Rust, For In Self We Trust.* In our current culture, self reigns. Everything is about self. When Israel became preoccupied with selfish desires and with the worship of idols, the prophet Jeremiah warned the people: *This is what the Lord says: 'Cursed are those who put their trust in mere humans and turn their hearts away from the Lord.'⁶ 'Consider then and realize how evil and bitter it is for you when you forsake the Lord your God and have no awe of me,' declares the Lord, the Lord Almighty.'⁷ For jealousy and selfishness are not God's kind of wisdom. Such things are earthly, unspiritual, and motivated by the devil. For wherever there is jealousy and selfish ambition, there you will find disorder and evil of every kind.⁸*

As we continue in sin, God continues to withdraw His protective Hand against evil. Tragedies such as the Columbine High School shootings, the Oklahoma City bombings, children killing children, and children killing parents are just the beginning. Evil grows without God's restraint (see figure, The Loss of God's Blessings, at the end of this chapter).

The preceding paragraph was written during the writing of the first draft of *My Brother's Keeper*. That was over three and a half years before September 11, 2001, when our country was attacked in a savage and unbelievably horrific way in the tragedy of the World Trade Center.

It is clear we are living in perilous and difficult times; and unless we, as a people of God, begin to pray as never before, God's hand will continue to recede from His time-honored position of protecting this country. He is the same God today as He was then.

When God warned Jeremiah to stay away from His disobedient people Judah, He said it was because *I have removed my protection and peace from them.*[9] God can and will remove His peace and protection from our country if we continue to fail Him.

The Federal Emergency Management System, or FEMA, declared 112 disasters in a period of 4 years, from 1977 to 1980. From 2007 to 2010, there were 232 declared disasters, which means declared disasters have nearly doubled since 1977.[10]

As a short recap, events in recent years serve as red flags.

In April 2011, at least 336 confirmed (some say 600) tornadoes ravaged towns from Mississippi to North Carolina. On one night alone, April 27th, tornadoes measuring EF-4 and EF-5 roared through the South in what is considered one of the deadliest disasters in the last 60 years, with several hundred lives lost and thousands of homes destroyed. In Alabama, I lived through that night with my mother, not knowing until later that a town named Phil Campbell, less than 100 miles from us, was completely leveled. Only one month later, Joplin, Missouri, was also completely leveled by a tornado that is considered the single deadliest tornado in 60 years. In May 2011, the Mississippi River flood caused hundreds to evacuate, leaving many homeless. In May 2009, thousands fled their homes from the firestorms in Santa Barbara, California. Two years before that, in October 2007, firestorms in California ravaged hundreds of acres of land and destroyed hundreds of homes. In that same year, too, hundreds of individuals were affected by the devastation caused by the Seattle/Tacoma floods. On its heels, were savage ice storms that gripped the Midwest, with numerous deaths. And no one can forget that four years before that, in 2005, Hurricanes Katrina, Rita, and Wilma left behind enormous devastation in Louisiana, Mississippi, and Florida, while at the same time an untold number of tornadoes in the Midwest destroyed vast areas of land. Of great concern, too, is the dwindling financial reserves to pay for these natural disasters (damage costs to Katrina, Wilma, and Rita are 57.6 billion dollars, according to CBS News on December 27, 2005).

In September 2008, a major financial debacle left most of working America with only half their retirement savings. And in November 2011, unemployment is still over nine percent and continuing to climb. California has declared bankruptcy. Other states are on the verge as grim financial reports surface. But worse still, the United States itself as a country is technically bankrupt as well, with the national debt over 15 trillion and with no hard and fast government solution on how to stop it from rising still higher or finding a reasonable way to begin decreasing it.

Is God laying waste to our country because of our disobedience? Have we driven Him to say to us what He spoke long ago to His disobedient people Israel through the prophet

Jeremiah, *The Lord, the Lord Almighty, will carry out the destruction decreed upon the whole land.*[11]

There are other horrors too numerous to mention, but one in particular is worth noting, as it proves how far we are removed from God's blessings. Though the number of homeless is difficult to ascertain, the National Coalition for the Homeless states, "The best approximation is from a study done by the National Law Center on Homelessness and Poverty, which states that approximately 3.5 million people, 1.35 million of them children, are likely to experience homelessness in a given year (National Law Center on Homelessness and Poverty, 2007)."[12] Many are homeless by choice; but many are not. In whatever way homelessness has become so real for so many, whether through joblessness or by choice, people living without shelter in the richest country in the world is a disgrace. It is not the result of God's blessings but rather His displeasure.

How far will we try God's hand? At what point will we wrest ourselves from the perils attached to being a victim to more violence and unrest, especially the threat of additional terrorism? At what point will we stay His hand from more judgments?

On a personal basis, the absence of prayer has produced not only lives lacking in inner peace, but also an environment with little external peace. Nowadays even some libraries are noisy, instead of the quiet retreats they are meant to be in order to concentrate on the art of learning. It is the silence that is missing in our world. Life is crowded with sound. Sound comes from everywhere: At work, at home, at restaurants, at malls. Music blares. The cacophony of the world is one of the devil's best tools to keep people from silence, which is so necessary in cultivating a deeper relationship with God, with each other, and, importantly, too, with our selves. We cannot replenish our inner lives when our outer lives are filled with noisy distractions.

Prayer needs silence. We need to be still. To sit still. To be quiet. To allow silence to refresh us. Silence has its own sound. We must learn to hear its special voice. We must fall in love with it. We must become enamored with it. *Be still and know that I am God.*[13]

Getting in the spirit of true prayer is work. But it is the greatest work we can do. It is where we can become powerful, where we can take the initiative *to do something* about the world in which we live. We do *not* need to be victims. We can pray! God will do the work if we will do the praying. He will set into motion changes through circumstances and people. He will create *godly, extraordinary* individuals, individuals who will bring change to our morally and financially failing country. And, yes, His favor will reach into every area of life, whether large or small; whether it concerns the needs of an individual, a family, a town or city, the energy crisis, the weather, it doesn't matter—God's mighty Hand reigns supreme over all. He *can* fix it! *Is anything too hard for the Lord?* [14]

Dear reader, are you willing to sacrifice your life for the spiritual health of another? Is the moral and economic brokenness of our country enough reason to try? And this on a grand scale? One by one we can slowly but surely restore health to our land. Intense, devoted, willful, prevailing prayer at this time may make the difference between freedom slipping through our fingers or restoring it to fullness. True morality springs from within, from the human heart, and God changes hearts.

There is an old Talmud saying that says, *If you save a life, you save the world.* Everything begins with one: ONE step a time, ONE saved person at a time, ONE prayer at a time. ONE for ONE.

This is the confidence we have in approaching God: that if we ask anything according to His will, He hears us. And if we know that He hears us—whatever we ask—we know that we have what we asked of Him.[15]

No president of the United States can solve our problems. No United States Congress can solve our problems. No government can solve our problems. No country can solve our problems. Only God can solve our problems. Only God by the power of the Holy Spirit makes impossible things possible.

God is the Creator of heaven and earth. He is the ONE and ONLY solution to our problems. Unless we submit to Him, nothing will happen, nothing will change. God uses people. He uses men and women to bring to pass His desired changes.

Only God at work in human beings can solve the problem. And only through the prayers of His people, will God do anything at all. It is the fastest way to true health and restoration.

The question is: Will we fall to our knees in prayer voluntarily or will we be driven to it by still more of God's judgments, perhaps even worse than those already experienced? Will we accept God's challenge to pray, to build up a hedge around America by standing in the gap for others? Will we exercise our faith and our will in prevailing prayer so that when the Son of Man returns, He will find us, the members of his Army, full of faith?

Can we believe it is impossible for God not to answer our prayers if we pray with deep intensity, deep fervency for ten minutes a day for a period of two, three, four, or five months without fail for the lost souls God has laid upon our hearts? That He will then begin to heal this land? Let this *not* become true for us: *The harvest is past, the summer has ended, and we are not saved.*[16]

In Isaiah, God posed the question, *Can a country be born in a day or a nation be brought forth in a moment?*[17] This question could also read, *Can a country be born again in a day or a nation returned to godliness in a moment?* Of course not! But we can begin. And the rewards are great:

111

...whoever listens to me will live in safety and be at ease, without fear of harm.[18]

I will grant peace in the land, and you will lie down and no one will make you afraid....[19]

The Second American Revolution is a war not to be fought with guns against an enemy without, but a war to be fought upon our knees against the enemy within. We are Christians. We are the Second Pilgrims. We are the Second Chance. We are the Second American Revolution. *One-for-one. Together. United. We can pray!* Only on our knees can we start that Second American Revolution. Will you join this effort by responding to this call?

Blessed is the nation whose God is the Lord.[20]

[1] 2 Chron. 7:14, NIV
[2] *Onward Christian Soldiers*, English hymn. Lyrics by Sabine Baring-Gould, 1865; music by Arthur Sullivan, 1871
[3] Eph. 6:12, NIV
[4] Jer. 12:17, NIV
[5] Job 12:23, NIV
[6] Jer. 17:5, NLT
[7] Ibid., 2:19, NIV
[8] James 3:15-16, NLT
[9] Jer. 16:5, NLT
[10] FEMA, Declared Disasters (http://www.fema.gov/news/disasters.fema)
[11] Isa. 10:23, NIV
[12] National Coalition for the Homeless, "How Many People Experience Homelessness?" NCH Fact Sheet #2, August 2007
[13] Ps. 46:10, NIV
[14] Gen. 18:14, NIV
[15] 1 John 5:14-15, NIV
[16] Jer. 8:20, NIV
[17] Isa. 66:8, NIV
[18] Prov. 1:33, NIV
[19] Lev. 26:6, NIV
[20] Ps. 33:12, NIV

God's Cover When Holy Spirit Is In Control

Showers of blessing
Things go better
Things are easier

As Sin Increases, God Begins To Recede

Blessings recede
Stress and weariness increase
Things become difficult, even hard

God's Cover When Holy Spirit Is Not In Control

Blessings disappear, except for
personal blessings for godly Christians.

Loss of good leadership
Loss of wisdom, peace, and joy

Less And Less Holy Spirit = Chaos

Rampant Sin Brings God's Judgment =

Earthquakes
Floods
Tornadoes
Famines
Firestorms
Ice storms
Etc.

The Loss of God's Blessings

Extraordinary Living

13

The Way to a Happy Life

Blessed are those whose strength is in you, who have set
their hearts on pilgrimage.[1]

God has called us to become extraordinary people so that we can experience an extraordinary life. He wants to do extraordinary things through us, in us, and for us. It is only a question of permission: Will we let Him?

Would you like to go on an extraordinary journey with God? Following is a list of how life improves in quality the deeper we go with God. My experience with God went down to the deepest level during the season of intense prayer as my sister's keeper. This is also the highest level. When we deepen our time with God, we are actually going higher and higher into His vivid Presence. The depth of our walk can almost make us airborne! At the beginning, especially in the early stages of our Christian experience, we can categorize our life as ordinary. It includes the following:

Ordinary

Church attendance

Minimum prayer time

Striving

Achieving

Reaching UP to God

Doing good works

Working for God's approval

Later, as our time with God becomes more and more important, when reading the Bible is a must and prayer the prelude to every day, our life slowly rises to something more extraordinary.

While the ordinary aspects of our Christian experience are still the bedrock of our faith, now there is a movement of His spirit that looks more like this:

Extraordinary

Understanding that God reaches DOWN to you

Obeying His call to you

Spending more time in intercessory prayer

Reading the Word and loving it

Being available to God and others

Remaining faithful

Staying close

Practicing patience

Enduring hardship

Waiting with expectation

Watching with assurance

Resting with God

As these traits become more and more part of one's Christian character, as godliness grows, we may on occasion, as happened to me in the writing of this book, find ourselves in the Lap of God in such an intensely personal way that we have a true glimpse of what is the highest and deepest level of all, the one that probably precedes being in heaven. Here are the aspects that define this kind of a godly time:

Highest and Deepest Level

Having God's confidence
Having God share the secrets of His promises
Having God speak to you in many different ways
Enjoying great moments of His peace

At this point, a Christian has truly traveled a pyramid to heavenly living. So friendship with God follows this basic pattern: The more time you spend with God, the more imprints of His life become marked in yours. The intimate promises God makes during any close encounter with Him lift the spirit, for they are good news for the soul. They are positive rays that heal the body, mind, and spirit. The balance of our life is affected, as we escape the boredom of a routine existence. There is a big difference between God at work in you, and you at work for God. Allowing God the freedom to do and to be *in you* makes all the difference in living a truly extraordinary life.

God's copious intervention into our lives makes us servants of glorious impact with patience and faith pouring through our hearts that cannot be duplicated by any human experience.

No bird is so solitary as the eagle. Eagles never fly in flocks; one, or at most two, ever being seen at once. But the life that is

122

lived unto God, however it forfeits human companionships, knows Divine Fellowship.

God seeks eagle-men. No man ever comes into a realization of the best things of God, who does not, upon the Godward side of his life, learn to walk alone with God.[2]

---

[1] Ps. 84:5, NIV
[2] Mrs. Charles E. Cowman, *Streams in the Desert* (Grand Rapids, MI: Zondervan Publishing House, 1977, entry for December 20)

Appendix

Prayers For The Land

The Neighborhood Strategy

For all the law is fulfilled in one word, even in this:
You shall love your neighbor as yourself. [1]

Everyone lives in a neighborhood. The president, for whom we should all pray, lives in someone's neighborhood. The senators and representatives live in someone's neighborhood. Movie stars live in someone's neighborhood. And, Christians are sprinkled like salt among and between them all.

Prayers should be for *everyone.* Institutions are made up of people. Our lives are touched daily with the services of those who either protect, keep us healthy, guard us from harm, or guide us to be legally correct. There is much controversy within these fields, which is all the more reason to pray for them, but many good and

127

wonderful servants exist in these professions, too, and we need to be grateful for them: The medical profession, the legal profession, the judicial system, the police department, and the fire department.

This appendix lists prayers for those neighbors who have special positions and affect our lives on a daily basis. It is a LIMITED list. For additional guidance on who and what to pray for, visit your favorite Christian bookstore. They have some wonderful titles on prayers for just about any occasion.

I urge then, first of all, that requests, prayers, intercession and thanksgiving be made for everyone—for kings and all those in authority, that we may live peaceful and quiet lives in all godliness and holiness.[2]

This appendix then includes prayers for the following: The Church, the United States Government, the State Government, the City Government, the medical profession, the legal profession, the judicial system, the education system, the entertainment industry; and some special concerns: those widowed, divorced, handicapped, or homeless. Last but not least, prayers for the family and our precious future, our children.

Our youth are a sign of our neglect. Our children are the fruits of our self-centeredness and corrupt ambitions. They are the weeds we grew while we thought we were gathering flowers. Now we must pay the price. Now the few healthy children spread among the many who are not, must fear for their physical well being, their emotional health, and their very lives. Only by God's great mercy and strength can a true change be brought into existence.

Whenever you are led at a particular time for a particular person in this appendix, remember these prayers should be offered in addition to the generic prayer, not in its place.

NOTE: For readability, the prayers that follow are written using the pronouns "his" and "him" to indicate both male and female readers. This is not meant to discriminate against the female sex, for I am a female, but it is simply an easier way to read these prayers.

---

[1] Gal. 5:14, NKJV
[2] I Tim. 2:1-2, NIV

The Church

Pastor

Lord, strengthen the heart of my pastor. Give him the power to rise above the circumstances of his busy life. He is in the ministry to serve You. He committed his life into Your care. Keep him from being so busy that he forgets to minister. Give him the grace to accept interruptions, for interruptions are from You, too.

May he shine as an example in conduct, speech, love, faith, and purity. Give him the power to preach the true message of Jesus Christ, rightly dividing the Word of God. Keep him free from daily temptations, for in this age, temptations are stronger than ever, and the pressures greater to maintain a godly life. Insulate him from devious and capricious individuals. Instead bring him encouragement through those to whom he ministers.

May he strive continuously for a life filled with righteousness, godliness, faith, love, endurance, and peace. May no prejudice reign in his heart. May he be kind and patient toward all, especially in teaching. Above all, grant him deep strength and wisdom; and, for the sake of his mind and body, balance his busy life with times of leisure, fun, and genuine rest.

(Taken in part from I Timothy 6).

A Church Leader

Bless the leaders of our church. Keep them sober, self-controlled, and orderly. Give them the ability to teach and to manage their own family. Keep them upright, spotless from being affected by worldly pursuits, from the love of money, and from the desires of worldly success. May they welcome strangers into their homes as a witness and testimony to Your Son, Jesus Christ. May they show no prejudice or favor to those of position or financial means. Keep them from the temptations of the flesh. Keep their hearts and minds above the vices of common man and the world. Bless them with wisdom, peace, and joy.

(Taken in part from I Timothy 3)

God's People

> *...pray always for God's people.*
> *(Ephesians 6:18c, GNB)*

Grant mercy, grace, and strength to your people, Lord, to those who bear the name of Your Son, Jesus Christ. Fasten the truth of the message of salvation about them as a belt, maintain the breastplate of righteousness, faith as their shield, salvation as their helmet, and the Word of God as their Sword. Guide them unto all holiness as they practice godly living in Your strength. Grant wisdom, knowledge, and peace in all their ways and works. Let them not be ashamed of the message of Christ. May they speak with holy boldness, especially now, when the night appears so very close. Make Yourself real in them that they might shine as the stars of the earth, for soon they will shine as stars in Your Kingdom.

Yourself as a Member of Christ's Army

Fill me with Your goodness and mercy, Lord. Grant me the power and the strength to do my daily work, to live in peace and harmony with my family, friends, and co-workers. Guide me with knowledge and wisdom.

Above all, grant me an understanding heart that I might reach out at all times to anyone who comes into my life; let me never go in haste away from someone who has come to me. Grant holy boldness as required in giving out Your Word.

Grant me moments of absolute quiet, true moments of silence. Reveal Your Scriptures to me that I might grow in all true measure into the likeness of Your Son, Jesus Christ. Thank you for all that You will do and have done.

The Government

I urge, then, first of all, that requests, prayers, intercession and thanksgiving be made for everyone—for kings and all those in authority, that we may live peaceful and quiet lives in all godliness and holiness. This is good, and pleases God our Savior, who wants all men to be saved and to come to a knowledge of the truth. (I Timothy 2:1-4, NIV)

I pray Heaven to bestow the best of blessings on this house and on all that hereafter inhabit it. May none but honest and wise men ever rule under this roof.

(John Adams, second President of the United States, letter to Abigail, November 2, 1800, on moving into the White House.)

The President of the United States

The Current President

Lord, I pray You will give our president wisdom and knowledge in each and every decision he must make, whether it is great or small. I pray You will strengthen him with moral fortitude and sound judgment. Give him the ability to view every situation with correct insight. May all matters of state be handled judiciously and according to Your will. When faced with major difficulties, whether in a time of peace or war, I pray you will give him deep and abiding courage. May you give him the strength to uphold not only the letter of our law, the U. S. Constitution, but also the spirit of it. Guide, bless, and direct him moment by moment, hour by hour, each and every day, and I will thank You for it.

During a Presidential Election Year

Lord, my deepest prayer is for You to bring to this nation a man after Your own heart. Bring to this nation a man of God, a man who is unafraid to stand upon the Word of God. A man who is upright in all his ways. A man of character, integrity, honesty, and goodness. A man who can be a stable and godly example to our nation, to our citizens, and especially to our children. A man who is filled with courage, able to go against the tide in decision-making. A man of sound judgment; a man with extraordinary insight into all matters of state. Bring such a man to power, bring such a man into our lives, and let us give thanks to You daily for Your answer in bringing him.

An Elected Official

(Governor, U.S. Senator, U.S. Representative, State Senator, State Representative, Mayor, Member of the City Council)

May this servant of the people be reminded continually that he is indeed a servant, an instrument of the people, to represent with honesty and fairness all concerns related to public service. May You guide him into wise and stable leadership. Give him a heart for the people, able to sacrifice a private viewpoint in favor of one desired by his people.

Give him sound and moral judgment, the strength to stand steadfast against the pressures of lobbyists; and free from the prejudice that accompanies influential positions, especially financially lucrative ones. Grant him keen insight into all public matters. Give him rest and recreation to balance his busy life with refreshment and nourishment for his soul.

Policeman

Thank you for _____who is busy every day serving the public by working to keep our community safe from harm, safe from the many horrible crimes that go on each and every day. Thank you that you have provided him for our protection and assurance for a normal life. Protect him from those who would destroy him; namely, those who are not right in their minds, the criminals, and the drug addicts who are desperate to feed their habit, and so many others. Protect and keep him. Give him the ability to remain calm in dangerous circumstances; the ability to react quickly in emergency situations; to interpret and respond quickly and accurately in all situations. Strengthen him in all ways to do his job well.

Provide for his personal needs and those of his family. Bless him abundantly above all I could ask or think. It doesn't seem right, Lord, that those who are asked to protect us with their lives, have such a small return financially. Bless him in unusual ways so that he will find his job especially rewarding to compensate for the lack of financial success. And always give Him Your abiding peace.

Fireman

Lord, protect and keep our local fire fighters. Cover them with Your holy shield of armor that, though invisible, is stronger than iron, stronger than metal, more resistant to flames than anything made on earth. Give them the courage they need to withstand dangerous tasks, to perform uncommon deeds, and to approach their work with caution, knowledge, and wisdom.

Give them rest in their bodies, refreshment in their souls, and joy in their hearts. Reward them with good things in return for risking their lives for our sakes. To make up for the lack of true financial return, bless them instead in the quality of their lives by giving them richness and depth in their daily life.

Member of Armed Services

Protect, guide, and empower this faithful member of our country. Remind him (and also us, for we forget sometimes) what high purpose it is to defend and honor our United States. May he serve with dignity and pride. May he not dishonor this country by untoward conduct, especially in a foreign land. May the laws of this land be ever close to his heart, so that in all ways the pride of country will be held in highest esteem while serving. Give each and every one the endurance, capability, and strength to serve with honor.

And upon his return from any war, may you provide him with much-needed comfort and healing. Keep him from endangering or taking his own life. Instead, give insight to those surrounding him and provide immediate aid, the kind that will restore him to normal life. Bless him with his family and grant him true health and prosperity.

The Medical Profession

Doctor

(Surgeon, Psychologist, Psychiatrist, Dentist, etc.)

Thank you for Dr._____. Thank you that he is busy every day serving the public by working to keep us healthy. Guide his heart, mind, and hands. Give him an open mind, because there is always so much new information available. Help him to sift out what is good and what is bad. Give him the compassion and understanding he needs to bring comfort and relief to his patients. May he uphold the sacred trust extended to him by his profession. May he do his patients no harm. Give him insight into the illnesses of his patients, so that he may diagnose them properly with the knowledge he acquired through his education, but give him an open mind to the things that are new in his field, even tested natural remedies. Give him wisdom in the administering of medications. Bless him not only with wisdom but also with energy and strength, for the practice of medicine is often exhausting work.

143

Nurse

(or anyone assisting a doctor)

Lord, guide the hearts and minds of nurses everywhere, for they are so often overshadowed by doctors and fail to win the praise they so richly deserve. Grant them the strength and energy to perform the many tasks of nursing a sick patient back to health. Give them understanding hearts, so that they might serve with diligence, gentleness, and deep compassion. Let each and every patient feel the healing power of their care. Bless them with peace; and make their burdens light.

The Legal System

Lawyer

Lord, guide the heart and mind of my lawyer. Rouse his heart with joy to win a case for the sake of justice instead of legalism. Just because something is legal, doesn't mean it's right. Give him the desire to participate in reforming the law at the state level. Only through real change here can there be a change in the laws. May compassion and mercy be at the root of his endeavors. Strengthen and nourish him in the laws that are valuable so that he will be able to make good use of them in his work. Bless him and energize him and give him favor with the judges. Above all, may he become knowledgeable in Your sacred laws, which are before all things. May these lead him to an understanding of Yourself, so that You can guide him to a perfect heart of justice through Jesus Christ.

The Judicial System

Judge

Lord, ignite our judges with the desire for true justice and mercy. Let them put aside their feelings of power that often block a true movement in resolving a case morally and with an upright hand. May they not haggle with the attorneys; but instead let them deal with these servants of the law in an understanding and compassionate way; the two should be on the same side, looking to the spirit of the law as well as to the letter of the law, which is so often corrupt. Guide these judges into working with the state legislature to change laws that are both absurd and wrong. Ignite them with the desire for genuine reform, so that they might indeed make a valuable contribution to the law. Give them true insight into each and every case, let their judgment be fair and just. Especially guide them in Your law and Your grace, to the honor and glory of Jesus Christ.

Chief Justice of the Supreme Court

Lord, this is the highest legal authority in the land. Give this person Your full attention in bringing him a heart full of justice and mercy. Guide him with true knowledge, true understanding, and sincere compassion. Give him an unwavering desire to rule with justice instead of by popular opinion. Should a judge rule by the decree of the people? Should not a judge look unto You, our Lord, who is the Great Judge of all the judges? Convict him of the poverty of his faith. Return him to the great principles of the Bible, and by so doing, enlarge his determination to uphold the U.S. Constitution without compromise. Guide his thoughts each day, granting reflection on the Wisdom of the Ages, Your Son, Jesus Christ. May He come to rule by Your Will so that his judgments will be made with a true and perfect heart.

The Education System

Leader in School System

(Superintendent, Principal, Assistant Principal, School Board President, Member of the School Board)

Give this person wisdom and understanding in exercising leadership over the teachers and staff in the school system. Give him a heart of compassion for the teachers. Give him the ability to build trust with his teachers, to establish a better working partnership with them.

Keep him from micromanaging but let him show concern for a teacher's *way of teaching*, instead of just caring about their attendance and punctuality. Do not allow him to be so bureaucratic that a teacher's spirit suffers by it. May the teacher's voice be heard above the din of rule-oriented bureaucrats. May he include them in the making of administrative policies that affect the school.

And guide and direct him with wisdom, knowledge, and patience in the making of those new policies and procedures.

May he exhibit fairness, respect, and commitment to any students who are problematic and need help.

And finally, may he support his teachers in front of students, so that the line of authority is properly maintained. Above all, may he look to You, who is our great Guide in all things, the One who knows best how to lead and how to build.

Teacher

Give the teachers in our city a special blessing as they educate our children. Guide them in their hearts and minds. Give them wisdom and understanding and the strength to bear all the degradation that so often goes with the job these days. Keep them free from anxiety and panic. Give them the patience to deal lovingly with unruly and unlovely children. Make them instruments of inspiration to their students instead of dread. Give them the ability to build trust with their students.

Give new strength, energy, and creative insight into their daily teaching. Keep them from disenchantment with teaching and the school system of today. Revive their desires to teach and strengthen them in this resolve.

Send special children into their midst that will encourage their hearts. Give them peace in their circumstances and envelop them with your tender loving care. Carry them on the wings of Your love, on the wings of Your spirit. Protect and keep them each and every day, and fill them with Your peace.

Special Concerns

Widowed

Lord, when we lose someone close to us, someone who is the center of our lives, the one who makes our days shine with sunlight and hope and peace, the someone who is our life's companion, our soul's breath, our heart's beat, when that someone dies, we are shattered into a million fragments. It is as if we cease to exist. We would rather go to where they are than stay behind alone.

(_____) needs you, Lord. He needs a close, personal relationship with You. Guide him to Yourself. Give him the desire for Yourself, Your Word, Your guidance. Bring him the peace he seeks so much. I plead the blood of Jesus over him right now. Cover him with the cleansing, healing, powerful blood of Jesus Christ, the Savior of the world. Bind up those unseen rulers of the universe that come so easily to one in deepest grief. Release him from any bondage to these powerful forces that would wreak havoc with his heart and soul. They have nothing in him, Lord. NOTHING! In the name of the Living God, Jesus Christ, I renounce them in him.

As the Holy Spirit removes the clutter of those awful forces, may Your peace flow into his heart and mind. I claim a complete healing and restoration for his heart and mind. I claim Your joy and peace.

May he become anchored in You, in whom there can never be a turning, or an ending, or anything but stability and peace. Praise God! In Jesus name, Amen and Amen.

Divorced

The anguish caused by divorce is often so much worse than the anguish caused by death. In death, the door closes. In divorce, the door remains open. It is an open sore that causes shame. We know how you feel about divorce, Lord, and yet today it is a raging disease set out to destroy the family. Sometimes blame is placed by others on the innocent member of a marriage. Be with this person. Grant compassion and mercy in how they are treated by others, for no one is perfect. You did not call us to be perfect or judgmental. You called us to be merciful and kind, to be examples of Yourself. It is You who told the woman caught in adultery, *Neither do I condemn you. Go and sin no more. (John 8:11, NKJV).* Let us equally view with understanding and compassion those who are less fortunate, who must separate from their mates and go the track alone. Guide, bless, protect and keep this individual strong. Refresh and nourish them. Renew and remake them into creative and blossoming individuals.

Handicapped

Lord, we are so blessed. We can see; we can hear; we are mobile. We are well and we are normal. Thank you, Lord, for your providence in keeping our physical being filled with life's richest blessings.

Guide those who are disadvantaged, who cannot see, hear, or walk. When You were on earth, You healed the blind and the lame. Give us the courage to pray big prayers for those who are in this kind of need. Give us holy boldness in prayer! Make us instruments of blessing.

Give those in need, special sight, special hearing, special mobility. Guide them with Your tender love, Your mercy, and Your strength. Bless them in unusual ways. Return to them blessings they cannot hold. And we will give You all the praise.

Homeless or Needy

He defended the cause of the poor and needy, and so all went well (with him). (Jeremiah 22:16, NIV)

He that hath pity upon the poor lendeth unto the Lord, and that which he hath given will he pay him again. (Proverbs 19:17, KJV)

Lord, guide us in our care for those who are poor. Give us hearts of compassion for them. Open our hearts to help them through ministries already in place, and give us wisdom to establish new ways to overcome their plight.

Be with those who are poor. We are too steeped in our wealth to know what true poverty means, but in the poverty of the poor, make them rich with Your blessings. Provide shelter and food and in the midst of their pain, bring them joy and peace; make their days bearable and full of hope for a brighter future. Bless them abundantly above all we could ask or think.

The Entertainment Industry

Next to a caring parent, the entertainment industry has probably the biggest influence in shaping a child's mind than anything else in our modern way of life. To become an effective intercessor, watch the shows you believe are harmful. Get the name of the producer, director, writer. Put yourself on the line for that person.

God will give you amazing results that will become visible, just watch! You might find yourself turning on the TV at an odd moment to catch a talk show revealing that so-and-so has been fired or been taken ill or moved out of the picture in some way. Or, better yet, that person has started reading the Bible. It can go like that.

Head of Studio or Network

No one is powerful next to you, Lord. You are the Creator of the Universe, so what can a man making a movie do in comparison to You? Yet these movie moguls behave as though all power belonged to them. Humble those in these positions who are in need of humility. Bring them into those places in their lives that will contribute to building a humble heart. Make them contrite in their wayward ways of leading millions of viewers astray with wrong ideas for living. *A broken and contrite heart, O God, you will not despise. (Psalm 51:17, NIV).* Make them ashamed of their immoral standards. Convict them of their sins. May they repent, and in their disgrace, turn to You, the Living God, who will not only heal them but restore true self-esteem into their lives.

Make of them examples for good. Feed their hearts and minds with creative thoughts and ideas that will inspire adults and children as well. Turn their lives around for good, Lord, and we will give You all the praise.

Actor

Give actors the courage to say NO to those films that weaken our society. Give them the power to stand against the rising tide of violence, immorality, and destruction. If enough actors refuse to work, the scripts will change. Only by saying NO to evil, can good begin to come. May they form groups to establish guidelines and principles that will nurture the growth of real values which are family-oriented and which can inspire for good the minds of our young people.

Writer

You are over all, Lord. You are over these writers. You know which ones produce which scripts. Choose for Yourself the writers You wish to promote and bless. They need our prayers. Guide and strengthen them in their resolve to produce morally inspiring scripts.

For those who are bent on evil, remove them from this profession. Give them the desire to go elsewhere or create situations wherein they will find nothing but blocked paths in their lives, until they succumb to Your hand directing them to stop doing what they are doing and begin to write meaningful, moral, and inspiring scripts.

Musician

Bless the musicians who inspire us with tunes that make our lives light and happy, that contribute to the nourishment of our hearts and souls. Strengthen and guide them in their work and bless their futures.

But, Lord, those who would produce sounds that are harsh, even evil, that grate against our nervous system, that make silence impossible, that create only unrest and disturbed thought, bring these musicians down! Bring them down and change their lives! They are destroying our youth! In the name of Jesus, work in their lives to bring complete change to their hearts and use them instead for good music that will inspire and uplift. We will give You all the praise.

The Family

Parents

Do not treat your children in such a way as to make them angry. Instead raise them with Christian discipline and instruction. (Ephesians 6:4, GNB)

Give parents wisdom and love in the raising up of their children. Give them the balance between necessary discipline and nurturing. Let them be strict but not overbearing. Let them be loving without breaking the line of authority between a child and a parent. Give mother and father time with their children, genuine quality time. Give them an ear with which to absorb the thoughts of their children. Create ways for parents to show respect and appreciation for their offspring. Give mother and father the patience and kindness in the midst of disciplining. Let mother and father be a moral example to follow. Let the morality of their lives come to be reflected in the lives of their children.

Let them ever remember that children are little people who need attention and nurturing, so that they might grow into nurturing, caring, attention-giving adults.

Children

Children are a gift from the Lord; they are a real blessing.
(Psalm 127:3, GNB)

Protect our children, Lord. Protect and keep them from harm and from harmful influences. Make their hearts pliable and willing to obey their parents. It is not a popular thing to discipline a child; the tide is against it. But Lord, give the children You have entrusted into my prayer care, the desire to obey, to understand that they are only children and must learn to listen to adults. Give them a trust in their parents. Keep them away from the harmful influences so prevalent today. Give them an iron will to withstand the onslaught of temptations to sex and drugs. Lift them above such temptations. Give them sound minds and hearts. Give them stability in the midst of the raging of their young emotions. Energize their creative spirit and bring healthy and strong influences into their lives that will nurture this spirit.

Give them respect for authority—for their teachers, their principal, and especially their parents. Bless and guide them each and every moment so that they might grow up to become worthwhile members of society. Even more, may they become trusted servants of the Lord Jesus Christ, so that they might become genuine blessings.

www.ingramcontent.com/pod-product-compliance
Lightning Source LLC
Chambersburg PA
CBHW060251050426
42448CB00009B/1616